C000132672

DOMINICA

Nature Island of the Caribbean

Edited by Arif Ali

HANSIB

Published in Great Britain 2009
Hansib Publications Limited
London & Hertfordshire, UK

Email: info@hansib-books.com
Website: www.hansib-books.com

ISBN 978-1-906190-25-5

© Hansib Publications Ltd

Images © Individually-credited photographers

First edition published by Hansib Publications, 1989

All rights reserved. No part of this publication may be reproduced,
stored in or introduced into a retrieval system, or transmitted, in any
form, or by any means, electronic, mechanical, photocopying, recording
or otherwise, without the prior written permission of the publisher.

Printed and bound in the United Kingdom

ACKNOWLEDGEMENTS

Thanks are due to the following for their support towards the publication of this 2nd edition of **Dominica: Nature Island of the Caribbean**.

First of all, to Prime Minister Roosevelt Skerrit and his government for commissioning the book; to Ambassador Charles Maynard who encouraged us to produce a follow-up to the first edition which Hansib published twenty years ago to mark the 10th Anniversary of Independence; to Hubert Charles, Executive Chairman of National Reunion Committee, and his staff.

To our team in the UK: **Managing Editor Kash Ali**, Project Co-ordinator Isha Persaud, Richard Painter, Ella Barnes, Alan Cross, Fidel Persaud, Chandani Persaud, Moti Persaud.

To the writers (in alphabetical order): Philbert Aaron, Irving Andre, Carla Armour, Alex Bruno, Alwin Bully, Aileen Burton, Brian Dyde, Lennox Honychurch, Ian Jackson, Arlington James, Edward Lambert, Marcella Larocque-Menal, Raymond Lawrence, Alick Lazare, Rhoda Letang, McCarthy Marie, Oswald Savarin, Dr Clayton A. Shillingford, Simon Walsh.

To the photographers: Ian Brierley, Irvin C. Durand, Lennox Honychurch, Dominica Festivals Commission, Simon Walsh, Cecil Clarke, Emeil J. Depooter Jr, Francis Richards, Prime Minister's Office.

And finally to Pamela Mary for caring so much.

Arif Ali

FOREWORD

It is often said that if Christopher Columbus visited the Caribbean today he will only recognise Dominica as one of the islands he encountered during his four voyages.

It is no wonder that the country is aptly described as the "Nature Island of the Caribbean". The country is a classic example of an ideal eco destination with adequate facilities to match most of the other Caribbean countries.

This book is meant to give an insight into Dominica for those wanting to visit, for those interested in investment opportunities, for the student and as a classic gift or memento for nationals at home or abroad.

The Prime Minister and his government are mindful of the occasion of the 30th Anniversary of Independence and have so commissioned this book, among other events, to mark this important date.

In a fast changing world, one can find it very easy to fall in love with this gem of a Caribbean island.

Arif Ali
October 2008

Message from the Prime Minister

It is with a special feeling of joy and delight that I forward these remarks to be included in this publication. More importantly, this provides another avenue to greet Dominicans in the Diaspora and citizens of our great homeland who have remained in-house to keep the ship of State afloat.

Indeed, thirty years is reason to celebrate as a nation but it is also an opportune time for reflection and review on how we as a people have faired on this journey since political independence.

The theme of our 30th Anniversary – Reunion 2008 – is very appropriately labelled "Celebrating the Journey Together." We celebrate because we have advanced as one people under God, in the words of the famous arranger Kenneth Morris, "through many dangers, toils and snares". In all of this we have learnt one significant lesson – "we perform at our best in all spheres of development when we do it together."

The thoughts and ideas expressed in this coffee table publication, the wide variety of features they embrace that sums up who we are, the history, the culture and craft the flora and fauna, the variety of cuisine, the nature and extraordinary landscape, complemented by our music and dance, presents that wholesome package of who we are as a people.

I invite all to celebrate this journey with us and invite you to come and share with us in this wonderful Nature Isle that we pledge to treat with tender loving care.

HON. ROOSEVELT SKERRIT

Message from the Minister of Tourism and Legal Affairs

Let me welcome you to the experience that is Dominica: A land that is fertile and green, rich in culture, steeped in tradition yet forever changing, yet forever beautiful. The magic of the Nature Island of the Caribbean is the magnificence of its mountain ranges, its free flowing rivers, its towering waterfalls, the charm and warmth of its people and its awe-inspiring natural beauty.

As we open up a new chapter in our country's history we recognise the need to build on our past successes, to continue the tradition of preserving what we have and being in control of our future. Our charm and our beauty are the essence of who we are and what make us special and unique.

In this latest publication on Dominica, I invite you to journey with me through our island, and hope that you will discover what those who before you have been privileged to see, feel, touch and smell. This book covers the diversity and the unique features of the island in the most stunning and compelling way that will make you want to experience it too for yourself.

Let me urge those of you who have not been as fortunate as others to visit this special and unique island in the middle of the Caribbean chain to look through the pages of this book and just imagine what awaits you. Come and discover the nature island of Dominica where each and every day is a different and special experience, and where each and every day we are challenged to take on a new adventure. Come and indulge in our beauty, our charm and our warm hospitality.

HON. IAN DOUGLAS

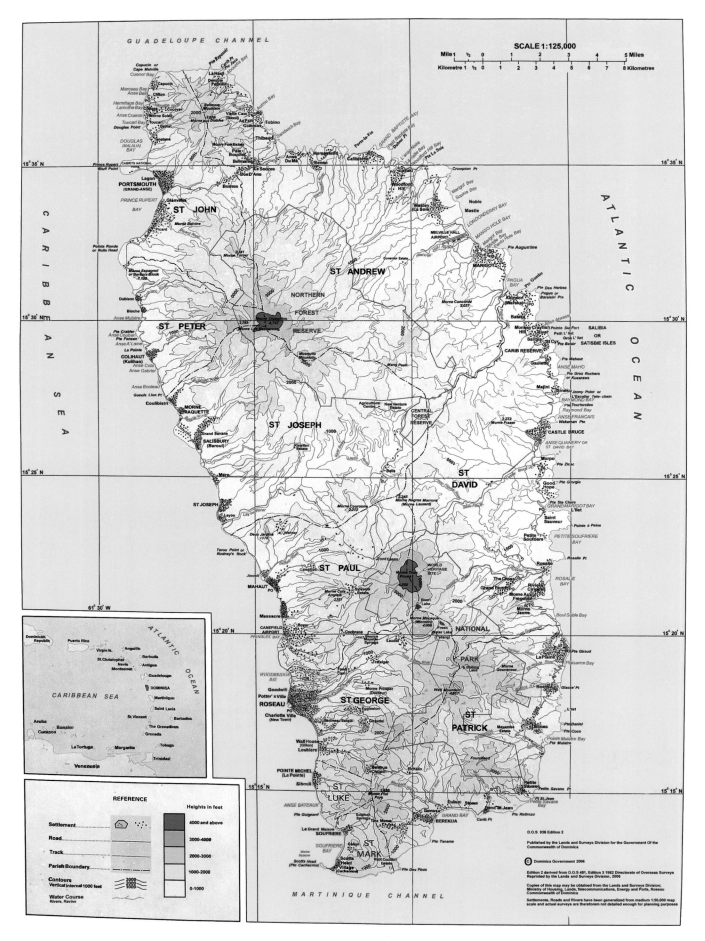

SCALE 1:125,000

| Mile 1 | ½ | 0 | 1 | 2 | 3 | 4 | 5 Miles |

| Kilometre 1 | ½ | 0 | 1 | 2 | 3 | 4 | 5 | 6 | 7 | 8 Kilometres |

REFERENCE

Heights in feet

Settlement..............

Road.......................

Track.......................

Parish Boundary........

Contours
Vertical interval 1000 feet

Water Course
Rivers, Ravine

4000 and above
3000-4000
2000-3000
1000-2000
0-1000

D.O.S 938 Edition 2

Published by the Lands and Surveys Division for the Government Of the
Commonwealth of Dominica

© Dominica Government 2006

Edition 2 derived from D.O.S 451, Edition 3 1982 Directorate of Overseas Surveys
Reprinted by the Lands and Surveys Division, 2006

Copies of this map may be obtained from the Lands and Surveys Division;
Ministry of Housing, Lands, Telecommunications, Energy and Ports, Roseau
Commonwealth of Dominica

Settlements, Roads and Rivers have been generalized from medium 1:50,000 map
scale and actual surveys are thereforem not detailed enough for planning purposes

FACTS & FIGURES

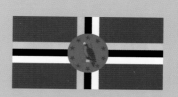

FULL NAME: Commonwealth of Dominica

AREA: 290 sq miles (751 sq km)

LOCATION: Dominica is a mountainous island of volcanic origin of the Lesser Antilles in the Caribbean, south of Guadeloupe and north of Martinique

POPULATION: 71, 180 (2006)

CAPITAL: Roseau

NATIONALITY: Dominican(s)

LANGUAGE: English, Kweyol, Cocoy

RELIGION(S): Roman Catholic 61%; Anglican 0.6%; Baptist 4%; Church of God 1%; Other Evangelical 7%; Jehovah Witness 1%; Methodist 3%; Islam (Muslim) 0.2%; Pentecostal 5%; Rastafarian 1%; Seventh Day Adventist 6%; Other 0.4%; None 6% (based on population census of 2001)

INFANT MORTALITY RATE: 12.3 (2006); **Life Expectancy:** 73.79 (male), 78.15 (female) -2008; **Growth Rate:** 7.4 (2006); **Birth Rate:** 14.9 (2006); **Death Rate:** 7.5 (2006)

INFLATION: 3.23 in millions EC$ (2007); **Unemployment:** 11.6% (2001 census); **Labour Force:** 8.4% male & 4.3% female (unemployed) / 61.8% male & 40.8% female (employed)

CURRENCY: East Caribbean Dollar (EC$ / XCD)

GDP: 467.71 (2007) in millions EC$ (ECCB)

GOVERNMENT: A constitutional, Westminster-style parliamentary democracy

MAIN POLITICAL PARTIES
Dominica Labour Party (DLP)
Dominica Freedom Party (DFP)
United Workers Party (UWP)
People's Democratic Movement (PDM)

HEAD OF STATE: H.E. the President, Dr Nicholas J.O. Liverpool

PRIME MINISTER: The Hon. Roosevelt Skerrit

ADMINISTRATIVE DIVISIONS (Ten Parishes)
St David, St Andrew, St John, St Peter, St Joseph, St Paul, St George, St Luke, St Mark, St Patrick. Forty-One Village Councils

PUBLIC HOLIDAYS
New Year's Day – 1st January
Carnival Monday
Carnival Tuesday
Good Friday

The National Flag

This is the proudest symbol of our nationhood. Hosted for the first time on 3rd November 1978 when we attained political independence. It consists of a circular emblem of red, bearing a Sisserou Parrot, the National Bird, standing on a brown twig encircled by ten lime green stars, each of which is bordered in yellow. This is superimposed on three vertical and three horizontal stripes of yellow, black and white forming a triple-coloured cross against a background of forest green.

The red central emblem symbolises Dominica's commitment to social justice. The ten lime green stars represent the ten parishes of the country, each with equal status, indicating the equality of our people. The triple-coloured stripes stand for the Trinity of God. The cross itself demonstrates our belief in God since the Commonwealth of Dominica is founded upon the principles that acknowledge the supremacy of God. The yellow stripes denote the sunshine of our land and our main agricultural produce – citrus and bananas. It is also symbolic of the Amerindians, the first people of the island. The white stripes symbolise crystal clear rivers and waterfalls and the purity and aspiration of our people. The black stripes represent the rich black soil of our island as well as our African heritage. The dark green background reminds us of our rich verdant forest and the lushness of the island. The flag was designed by Alwin Bully.

Coat of Arms

This is the symbol of our honour, pride and status in the world. It bears the inscription "Aprés Bondie C'est La Ter", which means, "After God it is the earth". It signifies the importance of the soil to the island, which has an economy based on agriculture. The design depicts a shield divided into quarters. The first quarter depicts the black volcanic soil of Dominica supporting a coconut tree; the second depicts the crapaud (frog); the third shows a Carib canoe on the Caribbean Sea; and the fourth features a banana stem bearing a mature bunch of fruits. A wreath of silver and blue and a golden lion standing upon a black rocky mount are at the top of the crest. A Sisserou Parrot supports the crest on either side.

National Bird

The Sisserou Parrot (Amazona imperialis) is the National Bird of Dominica. It symbolises our flight towards greater heights and fulfilment of aspirations. The parrot features prominently on the Coat of Arms, the National Flag, the Public Seal, the Mace of The House of Assembly and Dominica's Honours for Meritorious Service to the Country. The bird is among the oldest species of Amazon parrot and is found only in Dominica. It is now a protected species.

Easter Monday
Labour Day – First Monday in May
Whit Monday
August Monday – First Monday in August
Independence Day – 3rd November
Community Day of Service – 4th November
Christmas Day – 25th December
Boxing Day – 26th December

EVENTS

Carnival – February/March
DOMFESTA – Dominica Festival of Arts - May
Annual Gospel Explosion – May
African Liberation Day – May
Early Childhood Education Month – June
Sport Fishing Tournament – June
Dive Fest – July
President's Charities Annual Fundraising Dinner – June/ July
Emancipation Week –July/August
National Rabbit Festival – August
Nature Island Book Fair & Literary Festival – August
Creole in the Park - October
National Wob Dwiyet Pageant - October
World Creole Music Festival –last weekend in October
Independence Celebrations – October-November
National Cultural Gala – November 2
National Day Parade –November 3
The Dame Eugenia Annual Lecture (UWI) - December

IMPORTANT DATES

Independence from Great Britain – 3rd November 1978

MAIN ECONOMIC SECTORS

Agriculture (Crops, Livestock, Forestry, Fisheries); Mining & Quarrying; Manufacturing; Electricity & Water; Construction; Wholesale & Retail Trade; Hotels & Restaurants; Transportation (Road Transport, Air Transport, Sea Transport); Communications; Banks & Insurance; Real Estate & Housing; Government Services

EXPORTS (2006): 111,976 values in EC$'000

IMPORTS (2006): 450,619 values in EC$'000
 Source: Total Trade & Balance of Visible Trade – Statistics Division

MAIN EXPORTS

Agricultural / citrus, light manufacturing, quarried products

MEMBERSHIPS OF ORGANISATIONS
Regional

CARICOM, Caribbean telecommunications Union (CTU), Caribbean Tourism Organisation (CTO), Organisation of Eastern Caribbean States (OECS)
Hemispheric

Association of Caribbean States (ACS)
Organisation of American States (OAS)

Pan American Health Organisation (PAHO)

CARDI

IICA

CARICAD

International

UNITED NATIONS

World Health Organisation (WHO)

International Court of Justice (ICJ)

International Criminal Court (ICC)

International Maritime Organisation (IMO)

International Telecommunications Union (ITU)

United Nations Environment Programme (UNEP)

Universal Postal Union (UPU)

International Whaling Commission (IWC)

International Seabed Authority

World Trade Organisation (WTO)

Food and Agriculture Organisation (FAO)

IFAD

UNESCO

OPCW

ILO

WMO

WIPO

COMMONWEALTH

ACP

Organisation Internationale de la Francophonie

MAJOR TRADING PARTNERS

Export: OECS, Rest of CARICOM, European Union (2006)

Imports: OECS, Rest of CARICOM, North America, Central & South America, European Union, Asia (2006)

MEDIA

Press: The Chronicle, The Times, The Sun Newspaper

Radio: DBS Radio, Kairi FM, Q-95, Voice of Life, Radio Anba Mango

Television: Marpin Telecoms & Broadcasting (cable), G.I.S., SAT Telecoms (cable)

NATIONAL FLOWER: Bois Caraibe (Sabinea Carinalis)

NATIONAL BIRD: Sisserou Parrot (Amazona Imperialis)

NATIONAL MOTTO

Aprés Bondie C'est La Ter - "After God, The Earth"

TIME ZONE: GMT – 4hours

HIGHEST POINT: 4550 ft

INTERNET COUNTRY CODE: .dm

INTERNATIONAL DIALLING CODE: 1 767

National Flower

Our National Flower is Bwa Kwaib (Bois Caraibe) and is the flower of a small deciduous tree that grows mainly in the dry scrub woodland of the west coast. It is indigenous to Dominica and has survived our entire history and therefore represents the continuity of our people. Bwa Kwaib blooms in April and the bright scarlet flowers are displayed along the entire length of its branches. Its hardiness and scarlet flowers serve as a reminder of our strong and resourceful people who have the ability to overcome hardships. PHOTO: I.C. DURAND

National Anthem

Isle of beauty, isle of splendour,
Isle to all so sweet and fair,
All must surely gaze in wonder
At thy gifts so rich and rare.
Rivers, valleys, hills and mountains,
All these gifts we do extol.
Healthy land, so like all fountains,
Giving cheer that warms the soul.

Dominica, God hath blest thee
With a clime benign and bright,
Pastures green and flowers of beauty
Filling all with pure delight,
And a people strong and healthy,
Full of godly, rev'rent fear.
May we ever seek to praise Thee
For these gifts so rich and rare.

Come ye forward, sons and daughters
Of this gem beyond compare.
Strive for honour, sons and daughters,
Do the right, be firm, be fair.
Toil with hearts and hands and voices.
We must prosper! Sound the call,
In which everyone rejoices,
"All for Each and Each for All."

LYRICS: W.O.M. POND; MUSIC: L.M. CHRISTIAN

NATIONAL ANTHEM

Welcome to the Nature Island of the Caribbean

MARCELLA LAROCQUE-MENAL

If you ever thought green was jaded, then you've probably never been awed by the thousand shades of green found in Dominica. Known as the "Nature Island of the Caribbean", because of its largely forested and unspoilt terrain, Dominica is the most northern of the Windward Islands. "I cannot believe that in terms of grandeur and majesty there can be found anything in the world to rival Dominica's succession of forest-covered mountains," wrote Alex Waugh in 1948. "It is green, all green."

Dominica is the most mountainous island of the Lesser Antilles and is home to the tallest mountain in the Eastern Caribbean (Morne Diablotins). It is also one of the 'youngest' islands in the Caribbean as it is still being formed by geothermal-volcanic activity. This process can be seen at the Boiling Lake, which is the second-largest, thermally active lake in the world.

In 1493, Christopher Columbus visited the island and named it after the day of his 'discovery', Dominica (from the Latin word for Sunday). However, the island's pre-Columbian inhabitants – the Caribs – had already named the island Wai'tukubuli, meaning "tall is her body". Fiercely defended by the Caribs (or Kalinago), Dominica was one of the last islands in the region to be colonised by Europeans. Today, the country is home to the only remaining Carib population in the Eastern Caribbean. They are the descendants of the earliest human settlers in the region, after whom the Caribbean was named.

To acknowledge the significance of these first settlers, Dominica took the important step of protecting the landholding rights of the Carib peoples. In 1903, a 3,700-acre area was designated as a so-called 'Carib Reserve'. Known today as the Carib Territory, this protected region comprises eight small villages where the Kalinago people maintain their affinity with nature through knowledge and customs handed down from generations. Here, they continue to hone their

FACING PAGE
Screw's Sulphur Springs.
Often described as the most diverse in the Eastern Caribbean, Dominica's flora and fauna are equally at home alongside the country's many sulphur springs.

RIGHT
A characteristic Dominican welcome.

Photos: Ian Brierley

traditional skills such as canoe-making and basket-weaving. Although they co-exist quite comfortably in these modern times, they still remain committed to the spirit and culture of their ancestors.

Dominica's verdant landscape provides the perfect setting for an abundance of wild flora and fauna. Often described as the most diverse in the Eastern Caribbean, some species exist only in Dominica, such as the Sisserou Parrot, which is the national bird. The island is just as breathtaking beneath the surface where equally exhilarating adventures beckon. It has been rated as one of the world's top five dive destinations, and its marine life is regularly considered to be the best in the world. The waters around the island are also visited by seven species of whale, making Dominica the leading whale-watching destination in the Caribbean.

The Nature Island of the Caribbean is a truly unspoilt location. It has been said that if Columbus were to visit today's Caribbean, the only island he would recognise would be Dominica. This in no way suggests that the island is under-developed, but it has maintained its natural beauty and unblemished landscape.

Dominica is the real thing with no artificial ingredients and simply natural. The Boiling Lake is a prime example: to stand and peer over this bubbling crater means that you would be at least three hours' walk from the rest of civilisation. Eleven mountains afford hikers varying degrees of challenge; the island's 365 rivers crisscross the rugged terrain and feed into several spectacular waterfalls, the hikes to which vary from relatively easy to arduous.

Visitors to Dominica also have a varied choice of accommodation: from contemporary hotels, guesthouses and resorts to breathtaking wilderness inns and retreats where guests are woken each morning by a tropical symphony, performed by brightly coloured birds, amid lush vegetation and exotic flowers. In short, Dominica is a haven for eco-tourists.

Dominica is home to the annual World Creole Music Festival which celebrates "three nights of pulsating rhythms" to the sounds of cadence, zouk, bouyon, kompas, zydeco, reggae soukous and soca music provided by local, regional and international musicians. 'The Real Mas' is the Carnival festival that takes place prior to the Lenten season and hosts competitions in calypso and pageantry, and culminates in two days of street revelry. There are also many individual village festivals, such as Dive Fest, Emancipation Festival, Dominica Festival of Arts, Pork Fest, Rabbit Fest, Goat Fest, Fish Fest and Titiwe Fest, which celebrate the local customs, traditions and foods that thrive in Dominica.

Dominican culture is a rich and vibrant tapestry which is deeply embedded into the everyday lives of its people. And the people in question are welcoming and friendly; you can always expect to meet a Dominican for the first time and be greeted with a warm smile.

So come to Dominica to experience the nature, the friendship and the hospitality, and experience for yourself one of the Caribbean's best-kept secrets.

FACING PAGE
Bois Neuf Falls.
Photo: Irvin C. Durand

ABOVE RIGHT
The cascading waters of Diamond River.
Photo: Ian Brierley

The blanket-like
forest that covers
the island also
envelopes many
of the bays
around
Dominica.
Photo: Irvin C. Durand

Communities nestled within forested
terrain are located throughout the country.
Photo: Ian Brierley / Hansib

Pagua Bay on the
north-eastern
coast is within the
Carib Territory.
Ian Brierley / Hansib

ABOVE
The forests of
Canon in the
extreme north of
the island.

LEFT
Penville Falls.

FACING PAGE
An afternoon
stroll to Castle
Bruce.

Photos: Ian Brierley

ABOVE
Among the bay
trees.

LEFT
The road into
Soufriere.

FACING PAGE
A farmer
transports his
crop of bay
leaves.

Photos: Ian Brierley

St Joseph on the west coast.
Photo: Ian Brierley / Hansib

Colihaut in St Peter.
Photo: Ian Brierley / Hansib

A typical Dominican vista.
Photo: Ian Brierley / Hansib

The village of Dublanc in St Peter.
Photo: Ian Brierley / Hansib

The Dominican Diaspora

DR CLAYTON A. SHILLINGFORD

As early as the nineteenth century, Dominicans left the country in search of employment opportunities, but it was only after the Second World War that the pace of migration truly quickened. The early migratory period saw vast numbers of Dominicans going to the United Kingdom and the US Virgin Islands. In addition, over the past thirty years, Dominica has lost an astonishing fifty thousand of its finest sons and daughters to migration. The vast majority of this new emigration wave moved to the shores of the United States. Others have gone on to build lives in Canada, the United Kingdom, the rest of Europe, the US Virgin Islands, the French Antilles, St Maarten and elsewhere around the globe.

These emigrants may or may not hold citizenship in their respective host countries. Whether or not they do, they often seek the services of their home country, directly or through its representatives abroad (embassies, high commissions, consulates, etc) in respect to their own needs and those of relatives and friends. Many of these emigrants may eventually form households involving people from within or outside their national group, and create families of second and subsequent generations who, by extension, become nationals of the 'ancestral homeland'.

Some of these emigrants may return home eventually while still in their 'working years', and some may do so on retirement. However, as has been recognised by many countries the significance of this national resource cannot be ignored since the number of Dominican nationals resident abroad far exceed the population resident at home.

For a sizable number of Dominicans living overseas, there is a desire to reach out and assist their homeland. There is a stirring among those who have migrated from Dominica, and who are now beginning to understand and appreciate the role that they can play in helping make a difference in Dominica. They see the skills, experience and financial resources they have acquired effectively utilised in their adopted country, and recognise the even greater potential utility of these skills and resources at home.

This new attitude is at once astounding and reinvigorating. Scores of people are expressing a desire, not only to give back as they have always done, but also to go beyond that and take it to the next level. Like a wild fire, the vision for a new Dominica is being ignited and reinforced in the hearts of the faithful, and it is catching on. Like a nation taking up arms to defend its borders, a displaced people are rallying around a common theme to move its homeland forward.

Signs of that hunger and commitment were spectacularly displayed at the Dominica Diaspora in the Development Process Symposium organised by the Roosevelt Douglas Foundation, in collaboration with the Dominica Academy of Arts & Sciences which took place at New York's Brooklyn Marriott on 7th December 2001. Diaspora organisations and leaders from the United States, Canada, the United Kingdom and the Caribbean attended the event, alongside senior Dominican government officials and cabinet ministers Roosevelt Skerrit and Vince Henderson. For the first time in a very long time, the Diaspora was beginning to take stock of their circumstance and ask how they could contribute to 'nation building' in a more meaningful and structured way. Other initiatives such as the National Development Fund (NDF), assistance to the Dominica Cadet Corps, the Dominica Sustainable Energy Corporation, the Dominica Academy of Arts and Sciences (DAAS), Friends of PMH, and the runaway success of thedominican.net is further proof of a people wanting earnestly to give back to their country. The necessity of pooling the knowledge and networking competence of the overseas Dominican community for development projects at home has been realised most profoundly by the Dominica Academy of Arts & Sciences which led the way with its initiation of a skill-based directory in 2000. Under the guidance of Raglan Riviere, the co-founder and webmaster of the DAAS, many Dominicans — including the government — have benefited from this organised knowledge-based human resource pool. See www.da-academy.org.

FACING PAGE
Picard Food Court in Portsmouth is popular with students who attend the Ross University School of Medicine. The majority of the 1000-plus students are from the US and Canada.

Ian Brierley / Hansib

This willingness to help was well demonstrated in the work of the DAAS Diaspora Committee – in the detailed report it wrote, and in the voluminous survey submissions received. That report still remains an eminent roadmap of what we can do to enhance the role of the Diaspora in Dominica's development.

Over the years, Dominicans residing overseas have played a consistent part on an individual basis in contributing to the local economy. This support has usually involved the provision of financial and material support to family and friends, including help in migration, sponsorship, and in obtaining health care. In 1996, approximately EC $4 million was deposited in local banks by overseas-based Dominicans. In 2001, this figure had swollen to EC $12.1 million, and a further $1.5 million was sent through postal money orders. Contributions in kind also run into the millions. Several in the Diaspora have also contributed to the housing market through the purchase and/or building of homes in Dominica.

At the group level, Dominicans abroad are organised through various associations and social groups. Several such groups exist in the larger cities of the United States, Canada and the United Kingdom. Among the better-known groups in the United States are the Dominica Houston Association (DHA), the Dominica Association Mid-Western USA, the Dominican American Relief and Development Association (DARDA), the Dominica Association of Washington, D.C., CODIA in New York, and the Sisserou Club of Boston.

In the United Kingdom, there is the Dominica United Kingdom Association (DUKA), Dominica Bradford Association, and the Dominica Overseas Nationals Association (DONA). In Canada, the Commonwealth of Dominica Ontario Association (CDOA), the Sisserou Cultural Club of Ontario, and the Commonwealth of Dominica Association of Hamilton. In Europe, there is the Dominica Sweden Friendship Association, and the Kalinago e. V of Germany.

LEFT
Businesses in downtown Roseau. Over the years, Dominicans residing overseas have played a consistent part on an individual basis in contributing to the local economy.
Photo: Ian Brierley

RIGHT
Carnival in Dominica. For a sizable number of Dominicans living overseas, there is a desire to reach out and assist their homeland. There is a stirring among those who have migrated from Dominica, and who are now beginning to understand and appreciate the role that they can play in helping make a difference in Dominica.

Photo: Irvin C. Durand

Many Dominicans have also returned in a personal capacity to work, or to set up businesses. This has included retirees as well as younger professionals. The number of young people returning has, however, been woefully inadequate, with most opting to remain overseas after completing their degrees or professional qualifications. Those who return often complain of a system that is often hostile and not necessarily accommodating of their contribution.

While distance may lend enchantment to the Diaspora, it also allows some detachment and clarity of vision. Strong intervention by the Diaspora in the nation's economic life is unlikely to occur unless and until there are signs that the nation is serious in addressing these issues. The Integrated Development Plan (IDP) attempted to address some of these crucial issues, including that of institutional strengthening in the public and private sectors. It also proposed guidelines for social and economic development. Few of these efforts have until now directly incorporated the Diaspora as a factor in the national effort of economic transformation and national development. In 2004, Prime Minister Roosevelt Skerrit requested that the DAAS lead the way in crafting a Diaspora Policy Paper to provide a working mechanism for co-operation between our people and government, at home and abroad. Under the DAAS's auspices several notable Dominicans contributed to that effort and completed the paper. As of September 2008, however, there has been neither formal acceptance of the document nor systematic incorporation of its recommendations into government policy. While such delay is regrettable, it is still the hope of many that we will soon witness the acceptance of the Diaspora Policy Paper and the principle of progressive functional unity between Dominicans at home and abroad.

Despite the absence of such functional unity and the sometimes ambivalent relationship that might exist, the Diaspora has never been a lost branch of the Dominica family tree.

On the one hand, the Diaspora has been viewed as "deserters" who were not around to share the burden and grief of the home society in times of economic difficulty or natural calamity. On the other hand, it is regarded as a welcome source of public and private contributions of material and funds in both good times and bad. Visits by family and friends from overseas are always celebrated, participation in national events are always welcomed. Yet, those of the Diaspora who have

returned home and have settled on their hard-earned savings and pensions are too often regarded with resentment.

Whatever the changing circumstances and attitudes of residents at home, emigration and an increasing Diaspora will be a fact of life for some time to come. We would do well to examine how this part of our national family can be fashioned and influenced to the advantage of the nation as a whole. It is clear that other countries such as Jamaica, Ireland, Israel, Korea and India which have incorporated their Diasporas into national planning and development policy/activity have benefited greatly. It is our desire that our government and people emulate such success stories and do likewise.

The time is long overdue for our Dominica homeland, government and the public at large, to recognise the past and potential contribution of its sons and daughters abroad, and to welcome them to share as *full* participants in confronting and overcoming the challenges of the future. During this period, more than at any other time, we are faced with the necessity of maintaining a stable, civil and sustainable society at home and of promoting a national development consensus abroad. Dominicans at home and Dominicans scattered in lands overseas must join hands and hearts and voices across the intervening distances in a mutually respectful and productive solidarity. The fruits of such efforts are obvious. The Destiny of our dear land demands no further delay! ■

FACING PAGE
The Emerald Pool, with its cascading waterfall, natural pool and grotto, is a popular local hang-out.

TOP
Youths in Grand Bay show-off their tie-dyed t-shirts.

RIGHT
Boys at play in Soufriere.

Photos: Ian Brierley

Dominicans head for the
beach at the weekend.
Photo: Ian Brierley / Hansib

Keeping a
watchful eye
on his flock.

ABOVE
Police Force on
parade.
Photo: Irvin C. Durand

LEFT
Jing-ping
musicians.
Photo: Ian Brierley

FACING PAGE
Cadets in the
grounds of
Windsor Park
Stadium.
Photo: Ian Brierley

A peaceful moment on the banks of Indian River.
Photo: Ian Brierley / Hansib

TOP
Selling cakes
from her brightly-
coloured
verandah.

LEFT
A teacher in the
making.

FACING PAGE
Student nurses
in Roseau.
Photos: Ian Brierley

Two popular hang-outs in the Goodwill district of Roseau.

Photo: Ian Brierley

CABLE & WIRELESS

J B's Natural Fruit Juice

LEFT & FACING
PAGE
Street vendors in
Roseau.
Ian Brierley / Hansib

A vibrant performing arts scene

ALWIN BULLY

The performing arts flow through the lives of the Dominican people as naturally as the rivers through the landscape. Music, dance and theatrical expression have been the three supporting pillars of culture and the arts of which the country is justifiably proud.

In the 1940s and 50s, Mabel 'Cissy' Caudieron did pioneering work in this field by documenting many of the island's dying traditions and customs. Most importantly, she was able to bring home to the population the importance and beauty of the Kweyol/Creole language which she honoured in song and speech. Through her Kairi Artistic Troupe, she brought new prestige to this important aspect of the culture which at the time was in danger of extinction. This work was endorsed and bolstered in the 1960s and 70s by E.O. LeBlanc, Dominica's first Chief Minister and Premiere. LeBlanc played a pivotal role in the preservation of the folk arts through his establishment of the National Day Celebrations, which have evolved into the massive Folk Competitive Festival that it is today. This exciting and unique festival is held every year from September to November with competitions in all age groups throughout the island culminating in the Grand Cultural Gala on Independence Day. At this national event the finest performances are presented in the fields of dance, song, instrumental music, story-telling and myriad other forms of folkloric culture.

MUSIC

The folk music of the island remains the root of today's vibrant music industry. Coming from a long tradition of chante mas (carnival songs), work songs, wake songs, and songs within 'contes' in the story-telling tradition, this music has held a place of honour among the country's leading musicians who had enough foresight as to start recording them early in the 20th century. Fortunately, players of traditional music and their instruments have survived to this day. Drumming and the construction of various types of percussion instruments, the shack-shack or jing-ping band with its accordion, tambale, bamboo boom-boom and gwage, can still be found accompanying the quadrille dancers throughout the island. The Lapeau Kabwit drummers and Bele

FACING PAGE
Jing-ping bands are often found accompanying quadrille dancers throughout Dominica.
Photo: Ian Brierley

RIGHT
WCK performing at the World Creole Music Festival.
Photo: Dominica Festivals Commission

drummers with their chantwels, and the lead singers at wakes and religious ceremonies, all still form an integral part of Dominica's musical landscape. In 1971, folk music gained new recognition through the work of Jean Lawrence Mathurine and her Siffleur Montagne Chorale, which recorded an album of traditional and new folksongs. This led to the formation of several

FACING PAGE
The belè dance is one of the more popular folk dances of Dominica.

ABOVE
Folk chorales perform traditional Creole (Kweyol) songs.

RIGHT
Kweyol singer Ophelia has been entertaining fans at home and overseas since the 1970s.

Photos: Irvin C. Durand

other folk chorales with new recordings in the 1970s and continuing to today.

The chante mas evolved into calypso in the 1970s when young Dominicans began experimenting with new forms of musical expression, which they drew from the wellspring of the folk traditions. Gordon Henderson and his band, Exile One, created the cadance-lypso beat which developed in zouk music in the French islands, and more recently, the bouyon beat was created by Cornel Phillip and his WCK band. Also in the 1970s, Kweyol singer Ophelia emerged to take Dominican music to the world stage (as she still does today) where she is joined by her protégé, Michele Henderson. Led by the stalwart Norman Letang and the Swinging Stars Band – which has been playing Dominican music all over the world for fifty years – this island has produced more than twenty bands over the last three decades, many of which are now resident in the metropolitan capitals of the world. Bands like Gramacks, Billomen, Midnight Groovers, Black Affairs, Belles Combo, De Boys and Dem, Wooden Stools, Mantra, Roots Stem and Branches, First Serenade, Rough and Ready and Triple K, have gained international recognition as have other individuals such as esteemed reggae singer Nasio Fontaine and jazz flautist Free Joseph. Dominica has also produced scores of calypsonians and composers, many of whom (such as Pat Aaron) rank among the Caribbean's finest.

All of this led to the establishment of the World Creole Music Festival in 1996. Held on the last weekend of October each year, as part of the wider three-week programme of activities celebrating independence, this international festival now ranks among the Caribbean's best. It attracts bands and spectators from around the world because of its unique flavour and its celebration of Creole culture, and is a must-see for any music lover or culture enthusiast.

DANCE

Belè, quadrille, heel and toe, mazouk, lancers and waltz are some of the more popular folk dances of Dominica. While belè is practically unchanged from its West African origin, the others are adaptations of European folk dances created by the enslaved population in the 18th and 19th centuries. These

dances have survived in the towns and villages throughout the island and have become a main feature of the Independence Folk Competitions. Originally, they were performed in communal settings where the spectators would intermingle with the dancers and musicians in a joyous and celebratory party atmosphere. Ever since the 1950s, however, most performances have taken place on stage, mainly for the purposes of competition, but they are still best experienced in an informal setting of a village party.

In the 1970s, a number of creative dance companies developed, using the vocabulary of the folk dances as a point of departure but also exploring various other regional rhythms and traditions to produce what can be called a 'Caribbean creative technique'. Of these, the Waitukubuli Dance Theatre has been most successful. Under the leadership of Raymond Lawrence, this company produces compelling narrative dance dramas and abstract pieces with strong nationalistic themes. It also stages an annual season of dance which has become an important event in the national calendar.

THEATRE

The birth of Dominican theatre can be traced back to the carnival and story-telling (conte) traditions. The entire carnival is street theatre itself, but the humorous and satirical sideshows and 'Pappy-show weddings', which were performed on the sidewalks, actually used sophisticated drama techniques. The storytellers, on the other hand, use the 'call and response' convention to involve the audience in the fantasy; he shouts, "mesye kweek!" to which the audience responds, "kwack" to confirm their collaboration in the spinning of the yarn. Again in the 1970s, the Peoples Action Theatre brought these techniques into a formal theatre with a strong socio-political agenda. Founded by Daniel Caudieron and Alwin Bully, this group has branched into the Caribbean Theatre Network which regularly performs dynamic pieces along with Dominica's two other leading theatre companies, The New Dimension Theatre (under Steve Hyacinth) and Teyat Pawol (under Alex Bruno).

The performing arts and Dominican culture in general have been kept alive and have flourished through the work of a small but vibrant Department of Culture within the Ministry of Community Development, Information and Culture. It is located in the Old Mill Cultural Centre, a building which, itself, is steeped in historic and cultural significance. ∎

LEFT
Traditional
Creole dance.
Photo: Irvin C. Durand

Independence Folk Heritage Festival

RAYMOND LAWRENCE

Dominica's annual Independence Folk Heritage Festival, which includes the World Creole Music Festival, has now become the island's major festival, with activities spanning a six-week period from late September to November 4th. Activities also take place in all the various districts across the island.

The Independence Folk Heritage Festival is really a continuation of the National Day celebrations which were started in 1965 by the then Chief Minister of Dominica, the late Edward Oliver Leblanc, who felt that there was a need to revive some of the dying folk traditions and decided to introduce annual, island-wide competitions in most of Dominica's folk performing expressions. These competitions were a lead-up to Dominica's observance of National Day on 3rd November, which was the date on which Christopher Columbus sighted Dominica on his second voyage to the Caribbean in 1493.

So the National Day Celebrations continued until 1978 when Dominica became independent on November 3rd and from then the celebrations were referred to as the Independence celebrations.

During these celebrations, the competitions include traditional dances like Bele, Quadrille, Flirtation, Heel and Toe, Mazook and Waltz. There are also competitions in bamboo flute playing, jing-ping music, Kweyol song, creative dance, short-story writing, art and poetry.

Special highlights include the finals of the folk competitions, Dominica History Week, Heritage Day in a particular community, Creole Day on the last Friday in October, the National Wob Dwiyet competition, the National Youth Rally, Flag Day, Creole in the Park, the World Creole Music Festival, and Independence Day itself with the Parade of Uniformed Groups and the National Cultural Gala. Independence celebrations usually have a special theme and Dominicans take special pride in dressing up in their national wear which comprise the Wob Dwiyet and Jip for the ladies, and for the men, white shirt, black trousers, red sash with either madras waistcoats, jackets, or a madras band over the shoulder.

HERITAGE DAY

Dominica has been celebrating this day annually since 1986. Heritage Day begins what is described as Creole Week during the Independence celebrations. Heritage Day is held in a different community every year and the idea behind it is to highlight the particular community, its special characteristics and the special agricultural, industrial and artistic products of the community and community's cultural heritage. A special feature during the day's activities is to pay tribute to an outstanding cultural elder in the community. A typical Heritage Day programme starts off with a Creole church service, followed by an agricultural, industrial and artistic exhibition, followed by a cultural gala during which a cultural elder is honoured.

CREOLE DAY

Creole Day is a very special feature during Dominica's Independence celebrations. It is a day when Dominicans go back to their roots and dress in the national wear, speak a lot of Kweyol and cook mainly traditional foods in traditional style. On Creole Day one can expect to see persons from all walks of life dressed up in their Wob Dwiyet and Jip, and men's national wear. So in the banks, insurance companies, stores, restaurants and business places, one will see and experience various aspects of Dominica's folk culture.

The schools usually stage special activities with a national theme on that day and the majority of school children will be dressed up in their national wear. There is usually a Creole dress parade with hundreds of children and adults in Creole wear. The media houses present special features on Dominica's folk culture and all the news programmes on both radio and television are broadcast in the Kweyol language.

Creole Day is the climax of Creole Week which begins with Heritage Day and it is a total celebration of Dominica's rich folk culture.

NATIONAL WOB DWIYET PAGEANT

This pageant was introduced by the Cultural Division in 1982 to showcase and promote a sense of pride in Dominica's main national wear for the women – the Wob Dwiyet. The competition brings together seven young ladies from the various districts across the island and they appear in three different rounds of competition which are Performing Talent, Creole Spectacular Wear and Wob Dwiyet. The Wob Dwiyet Pageant is the only one of its kind in the region and has become a popular and integral part of the Independence celebrations.

WORLD CREOLE MUSIC FESTIVAL

The World Creole Music Festival is a three-day annual event at the end of October and usually features many of the leading musical groups and performers from the Creole-speaking countries and Francophone Africa. These groups include Kassav, Tabou Combo, Magnum Band, Exile One, Grammacks, Midnite Groovers, Ophelia, Michele Henderson and others. The festival is one of the few international events which focuses on truly indigenous music of Dominica and the Caribbean. It attracts thousands of spectators from Dominica and the Dominican diaspora and from neighbouring countries such as Guadeloupe, Martinique and St Lucia.

NATIONAL CULTURAL GALA

The National Cultural Gala brings together all the groups and individuals who have won competitions during the Independence celebrations. The gala is the grand culmination of the competitions and it is held on November 3rd – Dominica's Independence Day.

The Independence celebrations as a whole, play a very important role in helping to unite the country, build national identity and pride, promote and preserve the national cultural heritage and develop and promote the talents and skills of Dominicans. It supports many of Dominica's cultural industries including the arts and crafts industries, the preparation and sale of local food and the making and sale of Creole wear for both men and women. The occasion promotes education, cultural tourism, culture and agriculture, and recognises and honours the achievements of Dominicans in various fields of endeavour. It also helps to promote Dominica to visitors and the wider world while at the same time helping to build a patriotic spirit for growth and development among Dominicans and the Dominican diaspora.

The National Youth Rally.
Photo: Irvin C. Durand

An abundance of literary riches

IRVING ANDRE

Dominican literature reflects, to a significant degree, the island's complex history and extraordinary topography. Indeed, the works of its most famous writers, Jean Rhys and Phyllis Shand Allfrey, focus on certain aspects of this history and its underlying social and political conflicts following Emancipation in 1834.

Jean Rhys's classic, *Wide Sargasso Sea*, highlights the clash of cultures between Antoinette, a white Dominican, and her English husband. This clash ends tragically when Antoinette is ultimately locked up in a house in England. In a symbolic act of liberation, she burns down the house and is spiritually reunited with Dominica. In another novel, *Voyage in the Dark*, Rhys's heroine, who migrates from Dominica to England, is also haunted by her island experiences as she copes with a number of failed relationships. In a number of other works, including her partial autobiography, *Smile Please*, and her books of short stories, *Sleep It off Lady*, and *Tigers are Better Looking*, Rhys returns to her childhood experiences in Dominica between 1890 and 1906.

Rhys's preoccupation with Dominica and the ambivalent relationship between the local white population and the Black population is not unique. Phyllis Shand Allfrey's *The Orchid House*, like Rhys's *Wide Sargasso Sea*, is also based on the author's family life. However, whereas Rhys's classic is based on the post Emancipation period, Allfrey's novel traces the genesis of working class politics in Dominica in which she played a pivotal role in the late 1950s. Like Rhys, Allfrey manifests a strong identification with the local population, although an undercurrent of tension and ambivalence underscores the relationship between the two. In 2004, a small volume of Allfrey's short stories, *It Falls into Place*, was published posthumously.

Other lesser known writers have written imaginatively about various aspects of the Dominican experience. English traveller Alec Waugh wrote a novel entitled *The Fatal Gift* which focuses on the insular life of the small white expatriate community in the early decades of the twentieth century. Former Beatnik poet Royston Ellis has written a number of books, under the pseudonym Richard Tresillian, including *The Bondmaster Breed*, *Blood of the Bondmaster* and *The Bondmaster*, based on slavery in Dominica and a slave breeding plantation at Layou. More recently, Antiguan native Jamaica Kincaid has written *The Autobiography of My Mother* whose heroine, Xuela Richardson, struggles against the debilitating aspects of her Kalinago ancestry while striving to achieve a semblance of satisfaction in her life. Similarly, Marie Elena John, an Antiguan with Dominican ancestry, has written a novel entitled *Unburnable* which tells the tragic story of her American-based heroine, Lillian, who is haunted by tales of immorality and sexual degradation associated with her Kalinago mother and grandmother. Like Rhys's Antoinette, she resorts to an act of self-immolation which offers a physical and spiritual release from her tortured past.

Dominicans have also written extensively about the island. Father Clement Jolly has written a number of books including a novel, *The Rainbow Man* while his Trinidad-based sister-in-law, Dorothy Jolly, has authored a few books including a romance novel, *Heartaches and Roses*. Alick Lazare has published two volumes of short stories entitled *Native Laughter* and *Carib*. He has also authored *Pharcel*, a novel based on slave rebellion and resistance. Within the diaspora, attorney Gabriel Christian has documented his childhood experiences in *Rain on a Tin Roof* while his sister, Esther, has written about the archetypal search for love and fulfilment in her novel, *Chance Meeting*. Canadian-based Raglan Riviere, co-founder of the Dominica Academy of Arts and Sciences, has focused on colonial pretensions in his books *Rumpunch and Prejudice* and *Colonial Deception*. In *The Island Within*, Irving André has explored the repercussions of the conflicting loyalties of a Dominican migrant in Canada while in *Jumbie Wedding*, he focuses on the social distinctions and class pretensions of a small community in Dominica. Anthony Lockhart has exposed the dark underside of the 1970s Dread phenomenon in his novel, *Man in the Hills*. Other writers such as Giftus John, Jocelyn Royer-Meade and Julius Lewis in the US, Elsa Pascal, Gillis Simon and Paula Sorhaindo in the UK and Evelyn Musgrave, Eva Bruney and Patricia Joseph in Canada have all published small volumes of poems.

The genesis of indigenous creative writing in Dominica can be traced to the proliferation of literary clubs from the 1930s onwards. Creative writing received a strong impetus in the late 1940s largely through the pioneering efforts of Garveyite J.R.H. Casimir who edited four volumes of poetry between 1940 and 1948. Contributors included Dr Daniel Thaly, Dr Phillip Griffin, educators Roy Dublin, Albert Lawrence and Alexander Nicholas and future Dominican Premier, Edward Oliver LeBlanc. Since then, there has been three distinct phases of creative writing. The first commenced in the 1950s with the formation of the Dawbiney Literary Club. The organisation published a magazine, *Dawnlit*, which featured stories by writers such as Alick Lazare, Alfred Leevy and Cynthia Watt.

The ascendancy of Edward LeBlanc provided the second impetus for creative writing in the 1960s. The decade was dominated by the works of writers such as Alick Lazare, Dr Lennox Honychurch, Franklin Watty, Alwin Bully, Michael White and Dr Edward Scobie.

The march towards political independence and the Black Power movement in the 1970s provided the catalyst for the third phase of creative writing, particularly poetry. During the decade, a number of writers including Anthony Lockhart, Arundel Thomas, Dr Lennox Honychurch, Dr Emanuel Joseph, Mark Sylvester, Daniel Caudeiron, Giftus John, Leonard Joseph and Christabel LaRonde published modest volumes of poetry or short stories. In the ensuing decades, there has been an effervescence of creative works from a disparate group of poets including Dr Kay Polydore, Gregory Rabess, Ian Jackson, Augustus Colaire, Albert Williams, Delmance Moses, Alvin Malone, Peter Piper, Harold Sealey, Algernon Ducreay, Anthony Toulon, Helena Durand, Jenaud Jacob and Gerald LaTouche among others.

Thanks largely to the inspirational works of Jean Rhys, Phyllis Shand Allfrey and J.R.H. Casimir, Dominica's literary landscape now boasts an abundance of riches. ■

Pagua Bay on Dominica's Atlantic coast.
Photo: Ian Brierley / Hansib

'Mother' and 'Father' falls of
Trafalgar Falls are located in the
Morne Trois Pitons national Park.
Photo: Jan Brierley / Hansen

Looking down stream
from Trafalgar Falls.
Photo: Ian Brierley / Hansib

ABOVE
The water from Trafalgar Falls flows downstream through the rocks and bolders and is joined by water from the hot springs, left.

LEFT
Isulutaki Waterfall in the Carib Territory.

FACING PAGE
Bathing among the bolders and rocks.

Photos: Ian Brierley

ABOVE
Where fresh river water meets the sea.
Photo: Ian Brierley

LEFT
Bolive Cascade.

FACING PAGE
Most of Dominica's waterfalls are found inland but some flow off cliffs and into the sea.

Palm-fringed
shores of the
north coast.

Ian Brierley / Hansib

Archbold Tropical Research and Education
Center runs educational programmes and
lodgings for students at home and abroad.
Photo: Ian Brierley / Hansib

The Real Mas

ALWIN BULLY

The Caribbean's carnival traditions date back to the 17th and 18th centuries when the enslaved population was allowed to partake in the Christmas, New Year and Pre-Lenten carnival celebrations as practiced by the planter class. In those islands where French culture and Catholicism prevailed, the carnivals developed in the four days (Samdi Gras, Dimanche Gras and Lundi and Mardi Gras) leading up to Ash Wednesday and the Lenten Season.

One of the earliest references to Dominica's carnival is to be found in Thomas Atwood's *History of the Island of Dominica* (1791) in which he states that such plantation revelries would go on "for two or three days together, during which they dance the whole time, almost; but it seldom happens that their balls conclude without broken heads, bloody noses or some piece of perfect gallantry."

Upon Emancipation, such festivities extended themselves to the streets where a number of particular 'masquerade' (as it was called then) conventions were developed which are unique to Dominica and are still practiced today.

COSTUMES

Perhaps the most distinctive Dominica carnival tradition is the Sensay costume which has its roots in Ghana. When the formerly enslaved people were at liberty to mask and costume themselves, they naturally returned to the West African concepts of masking and self-transformation as practiced in tribal rituals and ceremonies, many of which have deep spiritual significance. It would seem, however, that in recreating these costumes in the Caribbean for masquerade purposes, for the most part, they were stripped of their spiritual aspects. While it is not unusual to see a reveller dance himself into a trance-like state, there is no clearly defined religious or spiritual philosophy connected with this carnival convention. The classic Sensay is made from sisal with wire mask and cow-horns but it also comes in stripped cloth, paper, dry banana leaves and in more recent times, frayed plastic and other synthetic material with or without horns. In 1963, these costumes were banned following a tragic carnival fire in which three prominent young men lost their

FACING PAGE
GO Girls Carnival revellers.

RIGHT
Costume band revellers.
Photos: Irvin C. Durand

Revellers dressed in Cloth Sensay.
Photo: Irvin C. Durand

Traditional Carnival Bwa-Bwa.
Photo: Irvin C. Durand

Revellers take to the streets on foot and in the most colourful modes of transport.
Photo: Irvin C. Durand

Photo: Irvin C. Durand

Photo: Irvin C. Durand

Photo: Irvin C. Durand

Photo: Francis Richards

lives. The ban was lifted in 1993 leading to a revival and new appreciation of the costume.

Other early costumes include the 'bwa-bwa" or stilt walkers; the Darkies and Red-Ochres with their black and red painted bodies; the Souswel-souwi or Bats; and the various forms of lampooning of the upper classes such as Pappy-Show Weddings and 'Tourists' bands. The national costume of Dominica – the Wob Dwiyet and the Jupe – were also Masquerade favourites. While these traditional costumes are still worn with pride, the modern carnival also flaunts the glitter and glamour, beads and feathers that have become the hallmark of most Caribbean carnivals, thereby allowing the old and the new to merge in a unique visual experience.

MUSIC

Carnival music started in vocal form with a Chantwel leading the band of revellers, responding to her call, to the rhythm of goatskin drums and other makeshift percussive instruments. These early 'Chante Mas', which functioned as a great social leveller and a sort of watchdog for social injustice, have evolved into the modern calypso of which Dominican singers and composers are among the region's best. The finals of the Calypso Competition are the largest and by far the most popular cultural event of the year. The street music is now provided by huge 'music machines' – trucks laden with massive speakers blasting live or recorded music to meet the dance demands of the thousands of revellers who flood the streets of Roseau on Carnival Monday and Tuesday.

The Carnival Season is a festival in itself, which actually begins several weeks before the final 'jump-up' days, with Calypso Tents and pre-carnival Fetes all over the island, which soon quivers with carnival fever. The excitement really begins with the official Opening Parade, which takes place two weeks before the main event. In that period there are various shows and competitions which are taken very seriously by the population often leading to heated controversies over judges' decisions and calypso lyrics. The Carnival Queen Show, with its

FACING PAGE
Dana Queen of
Carnival Band.
Photo: Irvin C. Durand

Lapo Kabwit band
Photo: Irvin C. Durand

Pan player
Photo: Irvin C. Durand

Photo: Irvin C. Durand

Photo: Irvin C. Durand

Photo: Irvin C. Durand

elaborate costumes and designer gowns, is another crowd favourite, as are the children's competitions, steelband shows and street 'blockorama's' in the final week.

Dominica is one of the few islands in which carnival parades are held in several towns and villages simultaneously. In fact, the visitor or carnival enthusiast can select his or her preferred carnival tradition and travel to the particular community specialising in that form.

The actual Carnival begins in the early pre-dawn hours of Monday morning for the Jour Ouvert (Day Opening) tradition when thousands of revellers pour onto the streets, most of them coming from the Dimache Gras parties and dances, many dressed in 'Ole Mas' comic or satirical costumes. It is also the time at which the Pappy Show Weddings appear. The predominant music for this event is the lapeau cabwit or goatskin drum band as well as the steelband.

In the city, by nine o'clock, the streets are usually cleared as the spectators line them in preparation for the Parade of Bands, which starts about an hour later. This parade is led by the Calypso Monarch and the Carnival Queen followed by other contestants, flag-wavers, drum majorettes, themed kiddies' and adult bands, and, sometimes, floats. It

travels through the decorated rectangular route along four of Roseau's main streets ending at about four o'clock in the afternoon when the streets are opened up for persons, costumed or not, to join the revelry until about ten o'clock. Carnival Tuesday, or Mardi Gras, the last day of Carnival, starts from about nine in the morning but really builds up in earnest from midday. The costumed bands on this day are usually traditional ones or 'gangs' dressed in matching t-shirt or print outfits. By three o'clock, the thickest crowds can have the entire route filled bumper-to-bumper with huge bands of revellers as the street dancing reaches fever pitch. The 'last lap' begins at about eight o'clock as the bands make their final rounds, ending at ten o'clock when the groups of exhausted but still exhilarated people start making their way home.

Among the Kalinago people, a symbolic burying of Va-val, 'the spirit of Carnival', takes place on Ash Wednesday.

Dominica's carnival is one of the region's best-kept secrets, catering mainly to its own citizens, its diaspora and French neighbours. Even then, flights into the island and hotel accommodations at that time are hard to come by. So, the advice to all those interested in experiencing carnival in Dominica, is to book early. ■

Crowds at the World Creole Music Festival create and electric atmosphere.

The year was 1997 and the place was the Dominica Grammar School grounds, more popularly known as "Carnival City". It was 8 pm on Friday, 31st October – Creole Day. The band playing was Dominica's Roots Stems and Branches (RSB) and the crowd of about 1800 spectators was in high anticipation, for history was about to be made.

And so began the World Creole Music Festival, a unique creation in Event Tourism in the Caribbean. What, you may ask, is so unique about a music festival in the Caribbean? After all, there were already a good number of jazz festivals in Barbados, Guadeloupe, Martinique, Grenada and Trinidad, not to mention the world famous St Lucia Jazz Festival. All of these events were specifically geared to attract tourists, so Dominica's entry was, on the face of it, simply a matter of following the fashion.

But the World Creole Music Festival *is* unique. Not only is it an event that was conceived and executed entirely by locals, but it is also, more significantly, the only festival that highlights and celebrates Dominican and other Creole artists. Even the well-known Reggae Sunsplash in Jamaica was conceptualised by non-Jamaicans! Dominica's festival has influenced the organisation of a surprisingly large number of similar events across the Caribbean. The organisers of the Congaline Festival in Barbados came to Dominica to study the World Creole Music Festival and then modified their own event based on our template. Similarly, for a number of years now, the St Lucia Jazz Festival has opened with an event that is a close replica of the World Creole Music Festival in terms of the acts that are staged. We also have had more than one attempt to put on so-called 'World Music' festivals with varying degrees of success.

The World Creole Music Festival has grown from strength to strength and has become the premier event in the Caribbean for Creole music at which artistes from all over the world yearn to perform. The festival has had performers from Louisiana, in the US, performing zydeco with their washboards and accordions; from the Democratic Republic of the Congo with their soukous and Afro-zouk rhythms; and N'dombolo and Coupé Decale from the Ivory Coast. The best local performers have always been prominently featured and they include Swinging Stars, Ophelia, Gordon Henderson, Exile One, Jeff and the Grammacks, Midnight Groovers and Michelle Henderson.

Dominica's Triple K have gained regional and international recognition.

© DOMINICA FESTIVALS COMMISSION

lude the scintillating kompa from Haiti,
formed by artists such as Tabou Combo, Top
te and Wyclef Jean who is better known in the
-hop world.

Festival organisers from all over the world
ularly come to the festival to scout for talent for
ir own events in Europe, North America and
e Caribbean, and a number of artistes have
ured contracts stemming directly from their
pearances at the festival.

As a tourism product, the World Creole Music
stival has fulfilled its role in attracting visitors to
ominica. It is estimated that the event regularly
racts a minimum of three thousand overseas
trons. While a thorough economic assessment
the festival has yet to be carried out, all
lications are that the event makes a considerable
pact on the economy. The last weekend in
ctober is one of the most eagerly anticipated
eekends in Dominica for tourism service providers
d the general populace alike. With Creole music
the air, Dominica gets ready to give their guests
rollicking good Creole time.

Although the festival is generally considered to
a spectacular event, many are of the opinion
at it can be an even bigger success by making a
w simple changes. One proposal which is under
tive consideration is the lengthening of the festival
om the present three nights "of pulsating
ythms" to a week, or an entire month. The
tended event would allow for a much more varied
rogramme that would attract a larger and more
verse audience and, therefore, significantly
creasing tourism and other earnings.

The World Creole Music Festival owes a lot to
number of individuals and organisations that had
e vision to see that Creole music could form the
asis of a world-class event. Chief among these
dividuals are the then CEO of the National
evelopment Corporation, Sheridan Gregoire and
lius Timothy, then Minister of Finance. Another
ey person was Gordon Henderson who was
valuable in getting the international media to
articipate in and sponsor the festival in its early
ages. Successive governments in Dominica have
ways strongly supported the event by making the
ecessary resources available. The festival has
ecome an integral part of the local landscape and
or anyone interested in the best Creole music in
e world there is no place better than Dominica
October.

Dominica's Swinging Stars is one of the Caribbean's
longest serving bands. They began life in the late 1950s
as the Swinging Teens and soon established themselves
as a breeding ground for musical excellence. Well over
75 per cent of Dominica's best musicians were part of
the orchestra and today, the Swinging Stars line-up is a
combination of veterans and new additions. As well as
being a national institution, the band has regional
acclaim and has provided accompaniment to such
notable performers as the Mighty Sparrow, Lord
Kitchener and Super Blue. *Ian Jackson*

PHOTO: DOMINICA FESTIVALS COMMISSION

ABOVE
First Communion
is an important
occasion for
these impeccably
dressed
youngsters.

LEFT
St George's
Anglican Church.
Ian Brierley / Hansib

FACING PAGE
The Cathedral of
Our Lady of Fair
Haven in
Roseau.
Ian Brierley / Hansib

FACING PAGE
A reflective
moment after
Sunday service.

TOP
St Anne's Church
in Massacre.

RIGHT
A place of
worship in the
Carib Territory.
Photos: Ian Brierley

ABOVE
Idyllic view from
Soufriere.

LEFT
Fishing nets in
Toucari.

FACING PAGE
Church in
Toucari in the
north-west parish
of St John.
Photos: Ian Brierley

Wesley Roman
Catholic church
in the northern
village of
Hampstead.
Ian Brierley / Hansib

Forest-covered
mountains create
an imposing
backdrop to the
town of Soufriere.
Ian Brierley / Hansib

MAIN PICTURE
Scotts Head Village, to the right of picture, looking north along Soufriere Bay towards Soufriere, as seen from Scotts Head. The thin strip of land separates the Caribbean Sea, left, from the Atlantic Ocean.

LEFT
Soufriere.

Photos: Ian Brierley

RIGHT
Scotts Head
Village is
Dominica's
southern-most
village.

Photo: Irvin C. Durand

Fishermen in Scotts Head.
Photo: Ian Brierley / Hansib

ABOVE
Fishing community of Fond St Jean in the parish of St Patrick on the south coast.

LEFT
Hauling in the fishing nets at Colihaut in St Peter on the north-west coast.

FACING PAGE
A well situated guesthouse.

Photos: Ian Brierley

Banana plantation in the parish
of St Andrew. Banana
production is Dominica's main
agricultural earner.
Photo: Ian Brierley / Hansib

Water and the Future

EDWARD LAMBERT

Rivers, valleys, hills and mountains; these words from Dominica's national anthem, convey a graphic picture of the natural heritage of the country Dominican's proudly describe as "the Nature Island of the Caribbean". The verdant green landscape, lakes, gushing streams and exotic marine life all thrive because of an abundance of that vital element: water.

Dominica is fortunate to have an abundance of water resources. Though river flows have decreased over the last thirty years, it is estimated that over two hundred million gallons of that essential commodity flows into the sea every day. This is in addition to groundwater resources, which current geologic findings conservatively estimate in excess of a sustainable one hundred and twenty million gallons per day.

The future economic fortunes of this island state is inextricably linked to the development and commercialisation of its water resources. It is estimated that ninety five percent of the population

has access to safe drinking water from a piped system. Currently, the government is carrying out feasibility studies to improve the water supply of the country's entire west coast and to provide the town of Portsmouth with a modern sewerage system. These investments will contribute to an increase in agricultural productivity, help to improve the housing stock and facilitate expansion of the vast tourism potential of the town of Portsmouth.

Dominica's forest reserves and water catchment areas are protected by various pieces of legislation that contribute to the sustainability of the resource. Vigilance is exercised to ensure that the integrity of the system is not compromised by the pressures of development.

The mandate to provide safe drinking water to all communities on the island vests in the Dominica Water and Sewerage Company Limited (DOWASCO). The company is taking the lead to more fully commercialise the resource and is examining the feasibility of water becoming a major foreign exchange earner. It is targeting the country's proven groundwater reserves to bring this about.

If the pronouncements of the visionaries and futurists come to pass, then Dominica could well emerge as the water saviour of the Caribbean.

Photo: Irvin C. Durand

The gentle rapids along the Layou River
are a popular site for river tubing.
Photo: Ian Brierley / Hansib

LEFT
Sari Sari Falls near La Plaine in the parish of St Patrick.

FACING PAGE
Syndicate Falls.

Ian Brierley / Hansib

Kubuli Bar in the
Carib Territory.

Ian Brierley / Hansib

ABOVE
Carib handicrafts
on sale in the
Carib Territory.

LEFT
Carib show
village in
Salybia.

FACING PAGE
Musician in
traditional Carib
dress.
Photos: Ian Brierley

Dominica's legacy of Creole wear

AILEEN BURTON

The encounter of cultures in Dominica, through European colonisation and the transatlantic slave trade, resulted in the merge of traditions and customs from the African, French and English communities. This mix produced our Creole culture.

One of the many ways in which this Creole culture manifests itself is in dress. Creole attire is a blend of European and African influences and contains elements of each in varying proportions. Eighteenth and nineteenth century visitors, like Italian painter Agostino Brunias, Thomas Atwood and Lafcardio Hearn, were so impressed that they felt compelled to immortalise our Creole wear on canvas and in print.

During the days of slavery, the simplest and cheapest form of dress worn by the enslaved Africans was the 'twa trou' or three holes, comprising a wide hole for the head and two others for the arms. This dress was made of a coarse fabric, usually sackcloth. Later, a skirt was added to the bottom half of the 'twa trou' and a length of cloth was draped over one shoulder and extended across the body to the opposite side and tied at the waist. A rudimentary headdress comprising a tied piece of cloth, and echoing its West African origins, completed the outfit. The term "Afriole" was coined by the Roseau Cultural Group in 1996 in an effort to give an identity to this ensemble, which reflects the transition from African to Creole culture.

The outfit of the Affranchi or Freed Slave of the 18th century is captured in the paintings of Brunias and Lemasurier. Whilst the attires of both male and female drew from European fashion at the time, there were adaptations. A spectacular feature of women's ensemble was the tall, cone shaped headpiece made from fourteen plain white or patterned heavily starched cotton head kerchiefs. A wide-brimmed, beribboned hat perched on the top for added effect, was optional. By this time, coloured printed cotton fabric was available and was purchased for the skirt and the several petticoats that went underneath. Similar outfits were worn at that time by the signares from Gorèe and St Louis in Senegal.

Coming out of the late 18th and early 19th centuries were the Gaule, Jip and Dwiyet. The Gaule

was originally a garment of leisure worn indoors. For example, after an important ceremony, such as a baptism or First Communion, the hostess changed into the Gaule on her return home to relax and mingle with her guests. This loose-fitting, ankle-length dress was gathered or pleated at the front and back and attached to a plastron. Plain or printed cotton fabric was used. Today, there is such a heightened awareness and appreciation of our Creole identity that this garment has been elaborated and is now used outdoors for formal occasions. The formal Gaule is made of white broderie anglaise or embroidered fabric with pleats, tucks, frills and richly worked sleeves.

When colourful madras squares reached the island, Creole women wasted no time in creating many different styles of headpieces for use with their various outfits. Here we find strong African roots pushing their way to the surface of the culture.

The Jip, designed by the mistresses of European planters to taunt their wives, was the most versatile, luxurious and provocative of outfits. The ensemble comprises a white decoltè blouse richly adorned with laces and ribbons with a plain or patterned

FACING PAGE
The Wob Dwiyet is the most formal and impressive of women's wear. Its multicultural influences are drawn from English, French and African styles.
Ian Brierley / Hansib

RIGHT
Performers are wearing the simple outfit which echoes its West African origins.
Irvin C. Durand

scarf or foula thrown carelessly over the shoulders or pinned to the back of the blouse with a gold pin. A white, starched cotton petticoat is also richly trimmed with laces and ribbons. For her skirt, the Creole woman chose brightly-coloured cotton or, depending on the occasion, silk, satin or velvet. Her madras headpiece, tied in varying styles with peaks, conveyed suggestive messages to the opposite sex. No expense was spared on gold accessories. Pieces of jewellery such as the *collier choux* were specially fashioned for this outfit. Thus did Creole women secure a niche for themselves in a socially stratified environment. They used every occasion to display creativity in dress and to be noticed in society. Their spending was excessive as each new outfit had to be more attractive than the last. The African spirit remained undaunted.

Finally, the most formal and impressive of women's wear: the Wob Dwiyet or Gwan Wob. Properly worn, it is breathtaking and the wearer, the epitome of elegance. A multicultural influence is evident in its evolution – the stateliness of the English, French chic and the flamboyance of the African.

The Wob Dwiyet consists of a full-length, long-sleeved dress. The hem covers the tips of the shoes at the front and extends at the back to form a train, tail or latchè measuring up to a yard in length. When walking the train is gathered up from the back with one hand and tucked under the arm in one swift, deliberate movement. Underneath is worn a wide, white cotton lace petticoat so heavily starched that it can stand on its own. A plain or printed triangular foula placed over the shoulders is secured at the waist ties. Bright flowered, striped, dotted or plaid cotton was the usual choice for

informal Dwiyets. For grand occasions, embossed satins or brocades were chosen.

The Dwiyet wearer or Dou Dou Matador as she is referred to, is meticulous. The rule of colour contrasts has to be observed and appropriate colours chosen for her particular complexion. One such Matador, Irenie Peltier, was often commissioned in the 1960s to present a bouquet to visiting dignitaries. She walked with 'gam' knowing that she looked spectacular.

The headpiece varied with the occasion. For informal functions the *tete revolver* or *tete cassè* is used, whereas for formal functions the *tete en l'air* or the *tete en l'air calendèe* (painted with saffron yellow stripes) was chosen. Gold accessories would include *Anneaux Chenilles, Vignes, Pommes Cannelles, Tété Négresse, Collier Choux, Grain d'Or* or *Chaine Gros Sirop*.

Creole attire is just as important to our male counterparts. Today, they have a variety of complementary ensembles from which to choose. A basic white shirt is complemented with a sash or cummerbund made from red satin or madras. Jackets, gilets and neckties of madras are versions to be chosen from to suit the occasion. These outfits were patterned on those seen in the paintings of Agostino Brunias.

The Jip and Wob Dwiyet and the male attire described above have been unofficially accepted as the national dress. Dominicans are proud to display and perpetuate their national dress on Creole Day, observed yearly on the last Friday of October. Heritage Day in the villages and Miss Wob Dwiyet competitions are other occasions for display. Members of Government proudly wear their national dress during Independence Celebrations.

Our Creole dress is spectacular and can hold its own in the international arena. The colourful fabric used and its sharp colour contrasts are true reflections of the sunshine of our "nature isle" and vivacious spirit and pride of its heterogeneous people. ■

FACING PAGE
Prime Minister Roosevelt Skerrit, in traditional Creole wear, dances the quadrille during the Cultural Gala.
Photo: Cecil Clarke

ABOVE RIGHT
Creole Day celebration. The term "Afriole" was coined by the Roseau Cultural Group in an effort to give an identity to this ensemble, which reflects the transition from African to Creole culture.
Photo: Irvin C. Durand

RIGHT
Creole attire is just as important to men, and they have a variety of complementary ensembles from which to choose.
Photo: Irvin C. Durand

The Boiling Lake is the world's second-largest, thermally active lake. To stand on the edge an peer into the soup-like waters is to witness nature at its most primeval.
Photo: Irvin C. Durand

Grand Bay.
Photo: Ian Brierley / Hansib

The serene waters of Indian River.
Photo: Ian Brierley / Hansib

ABOVE
Small bridges
throughout
Dominica traverse
the island's many
streams and
rivers.
Photo: Ian Brierley

LEFT
The ruins of
Dominica's
colonial military
past have
surrendered to
the forests of the
Cabrits National
Park.
Photo: Ian Brierley

FACING PAGE
Middleham Falls.
Photo: Irvin C. Durand

The cannons of the lower battery of Fort Shirley point across Prince Rupert Bay.
Photo: Lennox Honychurch

Dominica's bustling capital.

ABOVE
A 'Reunion 2008'
welcome to the
capital.
Ian Brierley / Hansib

LEFT
The arrival of
cruise ships to
Roseau provide
a welcome boost
to the economy.
Irvin C. Durand

FACING PAGE
The streets of
the capital seen
from Windsor
Park Stadium.
Ian Brierley / Hansib

Market stalls in
Roseau.
Ian Brierley / Hansib

ABOVE
Windsor Park
Stadium is an
impressive
addition to the
capital.

LEFT
The monument
on Morne Bruce
overlooks
Roseau.

Photos: Ian Brierley

ABOVE
Cruise ships line
up to dock in the
capital.

RIGHT
The High Courts
of Justice.
Photos: Ian Brierley

FACING PAGE
This quaint colonial building in Roseau now houses a boutique and a restaurant.

ABOVE
The president's residence in the capital.

RIGHT
Old colonial buildings in Roseau, far right, and Portsmouth, right, have been put to good use by local businesses.

Photos: Ian Brierley

The Old Mill
Cultural Centre
at Canefield.
Ian Brierley / Hansib

Canefield Airport.
Photo: Ian Brierley / Hansib

The perfect end to any day.
Photo: Ian Brierley / Hansib

Wai'tukubuli: Home of the Kalinago

LENNOX HONYCHURCH

On the north-east coast of Dominica is a settlement unique to the Caribbean region. Known today as the Carib Territory, it was established by the British in 1903 as the Carib Reserve. It was one place in the region where the descendants of the original islanders could maintain a portion of land after everything else – from Trinidad to Puerto Rico – had been taken from them. For thousands of years, their ancestors had roamed from the river valleys and ocean shores of the Guianas and Venezuela in lowland South America up along the chain of the Lesser Antilles to as far as the eastern islands of the Greater Antilles. Some sixty archaeological sites have been located around the island revealing stone axes, decorated clay pieces and carved religious objects dating back more than two thousand years. Here lived the people who gave their name (or rather the name that the Europeans gave them) to the sea and entire region in which we live today: The Caribbean.

But the Carib Territory is not the only home of the descendants of these indigenous Dominicans. East coast villages such as Good Hope, San Sauveur, Petite Soufriere, Petite Savanne and Bagatelle are also areas with indigenous ancestry and at the beginning of the twentieth century 'Caribs' were recorded living at Pennville and Vielle Case as well. Then there are many more Dominicans who may have Kalinago ancestry, but who do not look like or regard themselves as Kalinago people today. The point is the Kalinago ethnic influence among the Dominican population as a whole is much stronger than we would at first believe.

PLANTS, ANIMALS AND PLACE NAMES

We are also often unaware that as a group, Dominicans are the largest surviving community to use the Carib/Kalinago language in their everyday speech. Whether they came from Africa or Europe, or a combination of the two, our

FACING PAGE
Caribs in Dominica as depicted by the Italian artist Agostino Brunias in the 1770s.

RIGHT
Engraving shows Caribs trading with Europeans at Prince Rupert Bay.

ancestors adopted many words, particularly nouns and place names from the Kalinago. Many of our native trees and animals are still called by their indigenous names: coubari, acajou, acouma, galba, zicak, larouma are just a few trees and plants; agouti, manicou, touloulou, cirique, iguana, zandoli, calalli and sisserou are some animals; and Salybia, Bataka, Calibishie, Coulibistrie, Macoucheri, Colihaut, Sari-Sari and Sibouli are just eight of the sixty or so place names still in use.

Then we should consider the lessons that the Kalinago gave our ancestors about the uses of the natural resources of the land around them for survival. Their amazing knowledge was accumulated over hundreds of years about the wealth of the forest, the rivers and the seashore. These included the use of herbs for medicine, knowledge about which forest woods were best for what purpose and what was edible and what was poisonous. There were skills such as how to trap fish and shoot them through the water with bows and arrows, how to prepare and eat the river snail (vio), the lambi (conch) and chatou (octopus), and where to find the sea mollusc (bwigo). They knew where the best clays were located for making pots and how to process this clay by preparing it to be modelled and heated in open kilns. From childhood they learned which plant materials were best for making baskets, mats, hats and cassava sifters. Their gommier canoes have sustained Dominica's fishing industry for centuries. They showed others how to process manioc by grating the root tubers, squeezing out the toxic juice and heating the fibrous kassav on a griddle placed on three stones. Very important was their knowledge of the changes in the tropical seasons and the signs of an approaching hurricane. Because they had lived so close to the land for countless generations, the Kalinago instinctively knew the pulse of nature and how to live in harmony with its cycles.

The Earth was feminine and so was the island on which they lived. She was called Wai'tukubuli, meaning, "tall is her body". The Kalinago had no concept of the ownership of land, just as it is difficult for us to conceive owning bits of the sky or the sea. How could you possess that which you could not carry with you or take after death? They knew no boundaries. There was no concept of colony or nation state. As late as 1930, when Kalinagos were arrested for 'smuggling' from the neighbouring islands of Mariegalante and Martinique, they rose up in revolt because, as far as they were concerned, they were simply continuing to trade without borders as they had done for

FACING PAGE
Today's Kalinago regularly perform traditional music at cultural events and ceremonies within the Carib Territory.
Ian Brierley / Hansib

ABOVE RIGHT
Chief Auguiste was the first chief of the Carib Reserve when it was established in 1903. He is pictured with his wife.

thousands of years. They had roamed the islands as they pleased from Kairi (Trinidad) to Borinquen (Puerto Rico) moving from Wai'tukubuli to neighbouring Aichi (Mariegalante) and Karukera (Guadeloupe) on to Wadadli (Antigua) and Liamuiga (St Kitts). Caribbean integrationists are trying to achieve today what the Kalinago took for granted five centuries ago.

But perhaps the greatest achievement of the Kalinago is that they preserved the island itself for so long so that all Dominicans of whatever ethnic group can, over five centuries later, enjoy the benefits of the natural gifts which the land has provided. The defiant terrain of the island allied with Kalinago resistance allowed this to happen. Because of this, Dominica was the last island in the Caribbean to be colonised by European powers, and even then only the coastal areas were effectively controlled.

FIGHTING FOR THEIR ISLAND

By the 17th century, Dominica had become the refuge for Caribs retreating from the other islands where the surge of French, English and Dutch colonisation was sweeping them off their ancestral lands. The mountains, thick forests and rugged coastline provided a natural citadel for the final retreat. From this base they made defensive attacks on the fledgling European colonies that were being set up ever closer around them in Antigua, Montserrat, Guadeloupe, Martinique and St Lucia, pitting their arrows and clubs against guns and steel weapons. Fighting a rearguard action, they were attempting to forestall the conquest of this their last island. Further south, in St Vincent, their brothers were trying to do the same. For their pains, propaganda in Europe painted them as warlike cannibals who deserved to be swept from the face of the earth, or as Sir William Stapleton, governor of the Leeward Islands put it, "the necessity of destroying those Caribie Indians ... to make them flee to the Main [land], if I cannot compass their total destruction". Here on Wai'tukubuli they suffered at least two massacres in retaliation: one at Anse Du Mai in 1635 and another in 1674 at the village which, today, bears the name, Massacre.

The latter event was one of the most significant in Dominica's history. Thomas Warner, better known as Carib or Indian Warner was the son of the English pioneer colonist of St Kitts, Sir Thomas Warner, and a Kalinago woman from Dominica who was living in St Kitts. He was brought up in his father's household and grew to know the ways and the language of both the English and the French. When his father died he was about fifteen years old and his English stepmother ordered him out of the house. He ran away to Dominica and eventually rose to be the main chief of the west coast.

Carib Warner was determined to keep Dominica for the Kalinago people forever. Because of his background among the French and English in St Kitts he knew better than any person of Kalinago descent how to beat the Europeans at their own game. But it was a diplomatic minefield. The English in Antigua, led by his own half-brother, Phillip, saw it crucial for their plans of colonial expansion that they should get rid of him. On the other hand, the governor of Barbados, Lord Willoughby, thought that Carib Warner was more valuable to the English as an ally and made him Lieutenant Governor of Dominica. As it turned out Phillip Warner paid no heed to the Barbadians and set out for Dominica, where he murdered his sibling and massacred his village in 1674. The other chiefs on Dominica tried

to hold out and continued the resistance for a while, but it was in vain. Despite treaties of 1660, 1667 and 1748 declaring that Dominica was a neutral island to be left to the Kalinago forever, the greed to establish yet another sugar-rich island was just too much. It drove the French and English to establish plantations and fight over the island until the beginning of the 19th century.

As the forests were destroyed and plantations were established and thousands of enslaved Africans were imported, the Kalinago people drifted to the most isolated parts of the island to try to continue their life as they knew it. The British had long since given up any idea of making them slaves and they were allowed to do as they wished, or as the 18th century historian Thomas Atwood wrote, "they are permitted to roam wherever their fancies lead them, as much unnoticed as if no such people were in existence". They sold their baskets, canoes and game and fish such as ramier, pedrix, iguanas, mullet and crayfish to the plantations. With the money they bought hoes, cutlasses, cloth and rum, but otherwise they were self-sufficient and stayed away from the colonial plantation society.

THE TIDE OF CHANGE

Gradually, however, the effects of the new Creole culture that was taking shape on Dominica began to affect them. Their language changed and so did their religion and their personal names. When they were baptised by missionaries into the Christian faith they were given the surnames of their mainly French godparents, be they Valmond, Darroux, Auguiste or Frederick. One British Administrator, Hesketh Bell, was concerned at the threat that neighbouring squatters posed to the Carib lands and he established the Carib Reserve in July 1903

ABOVE LEFT
Sir Henry Hesketh Bell was the British Administrator of Dominica from 1898 to 1906. He established the Carib Reserve in 1903.

ABOVE RIGHT
Chief Irvince Auguiste in the 1980s.

LEFT
Chief Jolly John with his wife and daughter in the 1930s.

ABOVE
The entrance to
the Kalinago
Barana Auté at
Crayfish River
Falls.
Lennox Honychurch

to protect them. But times were changing fast. As primary schools were established and roads connected the Carib Territory to the rest of the island in the 20th century – bringing telephones, radios and consumer goods – the tide of change became a flood. Easier interaction with the rest of Dominica meant that ethnic mixing increased and the physical nature of people calling themselves Carib or Kalinago changed also. On a political level universal adult suffrage was granted in 1951 and it gave the right for every adult to vote in general elections without the qualifications of land and/or income which was previously required. For the first time many Kalinago people voted to determine the affairs of their island. In 1974, the Carib Territory, along with its adjacent village of Atkinson, was given its own parliamentary representative.

By the 1970s, there was a core of younger Kalinago people who had benefited from secondary education and who were following the indigenous empowerment taking place among native groups elsewhere in the Americas. They inspired others in the community to investigate their traditional culture and represent it in dance and song alongside the Creole culture that was being highlighted as part of Dominican nationalism. They began to adopt the original name that their people had called themselves before Columbus called them Caribs. Written as Callinago by the early missionaries it is now spelt Kalinago. This awareness movement gave birth to Kalinago cultural groups such as Karifuna and Carinia. Before independence, Kalinago leaders demanded that special legislation be made to ensure the future of their community and this resulted in the Carib Reserve Act of 1978.

For many years the Territory had become part of the tourist industry of Dominica as a place to visit to meet its people and buy their handcraft. In 2006, an open-air museum and cultural village was established around the Crayfish River Falls called the Kalinago Barana Auté (The Kalinago Village by the Sea). Here, the visitor can walk along a trail overlooking the roaring Atlantic Ocean that is part of the old Kalinago track through the coastal woodland. Displays and panels tell of the culture of the people and a special herb garden guides one through the variety of plants used for herbal medicines and culinary delights. Here, on this rugged corner of Wai'tukubuli, we learn about the survival of the Kalinago people through more than five hundred turbulent years on this island. The Kalinago heritage comes down to us together with archaeological remains, place names, language and ancient knowledge of the nature of this island which the Kalinagos have bequeathed to us all. ∎

Freedom fighters of the forests

ALICK LAZARE

Slavery in Dominica was not established until well into the eighteenth century. The tough resistance of the Kalinago (Caribs) had kept out the Europeans who continued to make several attempts to stake out small settlements along the rugged leeward coast. By 1745, when the French had finally succeeded in occupying parts of the north and west coast, there were only about 1,500 enslaved Africans on the island. Thirty years later, however, the number had increased to about 14,000.

There is no evidence that the slaves in Dominica were any more rebellious than those in the other islands, where slavery had been in existence almost a century earlier. More likely the heavily forested mountains and gorges did not permit contiguous plantations even along the coast and made it possible for runaway slaves to slip unnoticed into the forests, far away from the plantations. There they gathered in numbers in different locations around the island – Grandbay, Grandfond, around the lakes, in the heights of Colihaut, close to Belles, and as far away as La Plaine.

They formed themselves into camps and elected chiefs to lead them on raids against the European planters. These raids were partly in retaliation for atrocities suffered by some of them at the hands of brutal planters, partly to obtain food, clothing and weapons, and sometimes to free many of their fellow Africans who were still in bondage. These raids became so persistent and devastating as to rouse the concern of the colonial authorities. In 1778, frustrated that their militia was of little effect in bringing the runaways in, or even to contain them to the forest where they could do little harm, the authorities offered a general pardon and amnesty to any slaves that would return to their 'owners'. Of course, none of the runaways accepted this and the raids increased to such an extent that by 1790, thirty of the eighty plantations on the island had to be abandoned.

The ranks of the runaways continued to swell with whole families formed in some camps. They established a network of tracks that made it easy for them to cross the island in any direction and so elude any militia that was sent in pursuit. Many of these tracks are now being restored as the Neg Mawon Trail.

While the runaway camps provided for their inhabitants only the most rudimentary amenities, most of them were quite safe and comfortable to live in. Rev. Charles Peters, once Rector of the Anglican Church between 1799 and 1800, described one such a camp as "most romantically beautiful and grand; presenting, on a diminutive scale, a natural scene strikingly resembling the imaginary 'Happy Valley' of Abyssinia. It was a deep, spacious, and finely wooded valley, everywhere surrounded with summits so rugged, so lofty

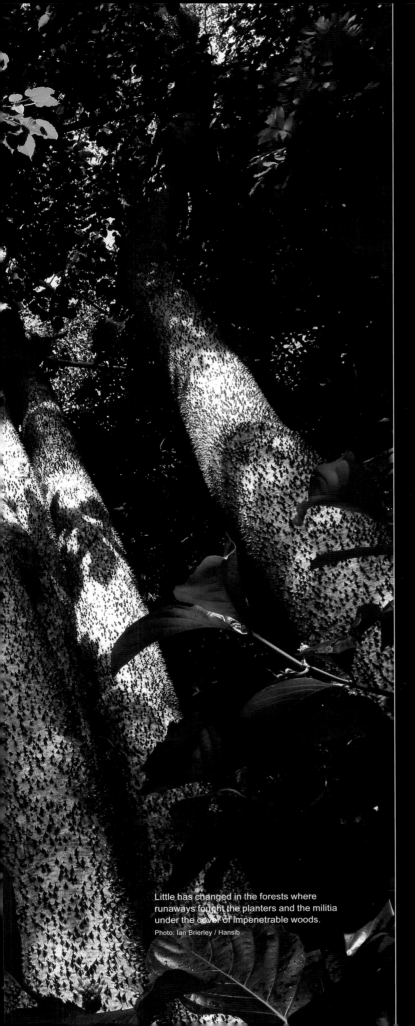

Little has changed in the forests where runaways fought the planters and the militia under the cover of impenetrable woods.
Photo: Ian Brierley / Hansib

and so precipitous, as to bar, apparently, all possible access to it. It had been, however, for many years, occupied by a considerable number of fugitive slaves, who had (at the time of this dispersion) cleared and cultivated such extensive tracts of its fertile soil, as sufficed to supply them in abundance, not only with the most nutritive roots and other vegetables, but with many of the most delicious fruits peculiar to the climate. After the treatment which (it is but reasonable to presume) a large proportion of those Negroes had experienced from their respective masters, can we at all wonder at the rapid augmentation of their numbers?"

A memorial of the Council and Assembly, dated June 1781, was recorded as follows:
"So little do the runaways stand in fear of being apprehended and brought to justice that they are daring and audacious enough publicly and in open try to infest the King's high roads and particularly between the Town of Roseau and River Mahaut, a distance not exceeding four miles where they attack, insult and rob passengers."

For nearly fifty years, the runaways fought the planters and the militia under the cover of impenetrable woods, using the precipitous mountains as an impregnable fortress.

It was not until 1786, after a devastating raid which virtually wiped out Rosalie Estate, that the colonial government marshalled a strong enough force, augmented by the planters themselves, to make inroads into the security of the runaways. Even so, the militia could not have succeeded as they eventually did had it not been for betrayal among the ranks of estate slaves and even among the runaways themselves.

Court records of the period 1786 to 1800 mentioned several of the chiefs, including Balla, Congoree, Coree Greg, Mabouya, Sandy, Hall and Jacco, many of whom with some of their followers, had been captured, tried and gibbeted alive. One of the most wily and intriguing of that group was Pharcel who at one time served as guide to the militia in exchange for manumission and a grant of land for him and his band. He was later imprisoned on suspicion that he sometimes served the cause of the runaways by forewarning them whenever an attack was to be made on their camps.

After 1786, with the execution of several of their leaders and the constant incursion of the militia in the forest, the strength of the runaways had very much diminished; but it was not until 1814, under Governor Ainslie, that they were finally and practically eliminated.

Official history has been unkind to the runaways, depicting them as brutal and senseless criminals. Today, it is hard to conceive the notion that any man should think that he had proprietary right over another or that a man should be branded a criminal when in honourable pursuit of his personal liberty.

The Kalinago were Dominica's first freedom fighters. After the Kalinago came the Neg Mawon. They left a formidable legacy of resistance against tyranny and a lasting desire for liberty and freedom that inspired the quest for independence.

Mission to recapture Fort Shirley

LENNOX HONYCHURCH

Overlooking the spectacular harbour of Prince Rupert's Bay in north-west Dominica stands the island's most important historic site. The Cabrits Garrison and its headquarters, Fort Shirley, cover some 260 acres on the twin hills of the Cabrits headland that dominates the bay. The iron cannons, which point out from the ramparts of this fortress, guard the town of Portsmouth, which was laid out to be the capital of Dominica in 1765. Today, pleasure yachts lie where the British Royal Navy once took refuge. Locally owned sloops and small cargo vessels bustle back and forth to the Leeward Islands carrying local fruit for the huckster trade. They travel in the wake of 18th century merchant sailing ships that once carried sugar and coffee to Europe. After more than 200 years, Portsmouth is now a rapidly growing community that nestles along the shore from Lagon to Glanvillia and beyond to Picard. Behind it rises a wave of forest green hills that climb towards the summit of the island's highest mountain, Morne Diablotin.

For over two decades, whenever funds have been available, masons, carpenters and bush cutters have been engaged at Fort Shirley recapturing the fortress from the encroaching forest and resurrecting the ruined buildings. Since work began in 1982, the project has received financial support over the years from the Canadian and British governments as well as from the former banana exporting company Geest Industries, the World Wildlife Fund and the Vernon Trust in the UK. After a period of inactivity, restoration was given a boost from 2006 with funding under the European Union Eco-Tourism Development Programme. This was followed in 2008 by the personal intervention of Prime Minister Roosevelt Skerrit who committed the government of Dominica to complete the restoration of Fort Shirley so as to house the Cabrits Heritage and Ecology Centre (CHEC).

The aim of the CHEC project is to provide Dominica with a centre for education and community activity where groups from Dominica, the region and the wider world can attend educational camps in an historic and ecologically preserved setting to learn about the environment and heritage of Dominica. Community groups, students – both local and foreign – artists, researchers in such fields as archaeology,

FACING PAGE
A cannon lies silent amid the ruins of the Cabrits National Park.
Ian Brierley / Hansib

RIGHT
Officers' quarters before restoration.
Lennox Honychurch

The restored officers' quarters has already become a venue for receptions, conferences, lectures and similar activities.

Lennox Honychurch

anthropology, botany and zoology can come and take up residence for a time and use the area as a centre for their activities.

The restored Officers' Quarters has already become a venue for receptions, conferences, lectures and similar activities. Fort Shirley now has a multipurpose use as both a tourism site and an active centre for visitors and nationals. All of this will help to make the place self-sustaining. It will be run by the CHEC Foundation, a non-governmental organization that manages the centre on terms agreed on by the responsible government departments. In this historic setting, with natural features of marine and forest ecology close at hand, the Cabrits provides an ideal location for the establishment of such an institution. The restored Parade Ground will provide a sports field for exercise and recreation.

Walking trails have been opened up along the military roads that linked all sections of the garrison. While Fort Shirley is being completely restored, the rest of the buildings, such as barracks, cisterns, gun batteries, slave huts, powder magazines and ordnance stores that lie in the forest along the trail, will be left in their natural state. It is unlikely that there will be funds to restore these as well. But historic ruins covered in the roots of strangler fig, and abandoned cannons peeping out of foliage, stimulate a mysterious and romantic spirit to the adventure.

The Cabrits headland is made up of the remains of a volcanic crater that erupted off the north-west coast of Dominica and was then joined to the main island by tidal sand and alluvial deposits from the nearby hills. The Cabrits derives its name from the Spanish, Portuguese and French Creole names for goat. Sailors would leave pigs and goats to roam wild on the headland so as to multiply to provide fresh meat on future visits to the bay. Later, it was also called Prince Rupert's Head after Prince Rupert of the Rhine who used the bay to repair and refresh his sailing ships in the 1650s.

The fortification of Prince Rupert's began after the Treaty of Paris had ceded Dominica to Britain in 1763. The first small battery appears to have been erected in about 1765. Military engineers identified the site as a strategic post to defend the north of Dominica from the French and for the protection of the Royal Navy when on call to refresh its ships with wood and fresh water. Major work began under the governorship of Thomas Shirley (1774-1778) who gave his name to the fort. Construction of the garrison was a sporadic affair from 1774-1825 with intense work being carried out during periods of enemy threat particularly during the American War of Independence, the French Revolution and Napoleonic Wars.

Although the Cabrits never saw action, it succeeded as being a deterrent to attack on a number of occasions particularly during the French invasions of Dominica in 1795 and 1805. The most important naval battle in the Caribbean – the Battle of the Saints, 12 April 1782 – was fought within sight of the ramparts. Fort Shirley was the scene of the famous revolt of the 8th West India Regiment in 1802 when African slave soldiers took over the garrison for three days in protest over conditions there and the fear of being sent to work in the cane fields. Their action resulted in all slave soldiers in the British Army being made free in 1807.

The British undertook most of the construction but the French made significant additions during their occupation of Dominica from 1778 to 1784. Together, they amassed a garrison comprising one fort, seven gun batteries, seven cisterns, powder magazines, ordnance storehouses, bakeries, iron forge, barracks and officers' quarters to house and provide for over 600 men on regular duty along with their support staff of artisans and slaves. With the end of hostilities between Britain and France, the garrison became obsolete and was finally abandoned in 1854. It remained in the hands of the British Admiralty until 1901 when it was transferred to the government of the colony and remained designated as Crown Land. Occasionally, it was used as a quarantine and agricultural station. It was established as a National Park in 1986 and is now destined to become an important centre for the study of small island ecology and heritage for the Eastern Caribbean. ■

FACING PAGE
Cannons on the upper battery of Fort Shirley.
Lennox Honychurch

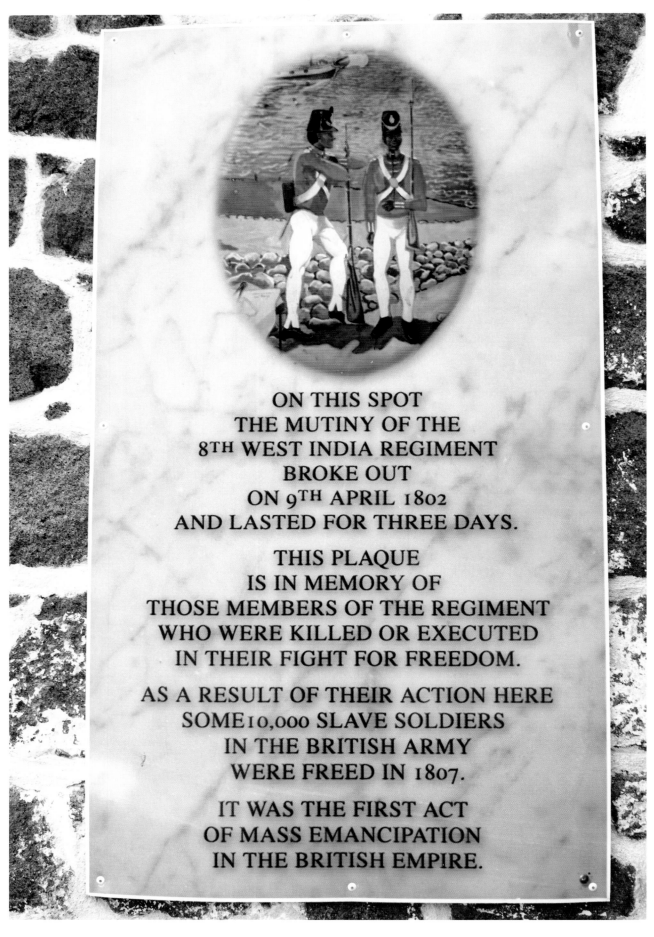

ON THIS SPOT
THE MUTINY OF THE
8TH WEST INDIA REGIMENT
BROKE OUT
ON 9TH APRIL 1802
AND LASTED FOR THREE DAYS.

THIS PLAQUE
IS IN MEMORY OF
THOSE MEMBERS OF THE REGIMENT
WHO WERE KILLED OR EXECUTED
IN THEIR FIGHT FOR FREEDOM.

AS A RESULT OF THEIR ACTION HERE
SOME 10,000 SLAVE SOLDIERS
IN THE BRITISH ARMY
WERE FREED IN 1807.

IT WAS THE FIRST ACT
OF MASS EMANCIPATION
IN THE BRITISH EMPIRE.

The Mutiny of 1802

BRIAN DYDE

owards the end of 1801, the 8th West India Regiment, which had been in Dominica for most of the time since 1798, was stationed in the north of the island in a fort guarding the important anchorage in Prince Rupert's Bay. Fort Shirley was superbly sited on Prince Rupert's Bluff, the hilly extremity of a peninsula which formed the northern side of the bay, separated from the mainland by a large area of marshland on the neck of the peninsula. Early in 1802, Colonel Johnstone received orders to have clearing and drainage work carried out in the marshes, in order to make the area more healthy and to improve the landward approaches to the fort. His orders contained specific instructions that, if Black troops were to be used on this work, they were to be paid the extra ninepence a day which white soldiers received when doing work which would otherwise have to be carried out by civilian labour. Johnstone was not a man to obey an order without first considering what advantage, if any, its execution might bring to himself. After entering into a syndicate which bought up uncultivated land in the vicinity of the marshes, he set the regiment to work in clearing access to this rather than in improving the outer reaches of the fort.

Long before the work started, Johnstone, as Colonel of the regiment and with the connivance of several of its officers, had worked out methods of defrauding the men by diverting regimental funds and keeping their pay in arrears. To even consider now paying each man an extra ninepence a day was out of the question, and the funds with which he had been provided to meet this expense were put to his own use.

While it is possible that the troops doing the work might not have known they were entitled to extra pay, they would have objected to such employment in any case. To be set to work with hoes, spades and billhooks went against all the effort made during their training to make them feel superior to plantation slaves, and they were immediately suspicious of the motives of their officers in ordering such menial employment. Their suspicions turned to fear and anger in March after

some of them had been in contact with slaves from the nearby plantations. The latter, who were understandably jealous of Black soldiers, spread the rumour that the 8th West India Regiment was about to be disbanded, and that the soldiers were being used as labourers in preparation for being sold to plantation owners. Those most affected by such tales were the men most recently entered into the regiment, and who were still far from fluent in English. With memories of enslavement, slave ships and slave masters not yet faded, any departure from the orderly routine to which they had become accustomed was bound to create doubt and unease. When half-understood rumours began to circulate among them, this unease quickly turned into panicky distress. The arrival of two warships in Prince Rupert's Bay on 9th April brought matters to a head. During their day's work the story circulated that the ships had come to carry them away into plantation slavery, and on return to their barracks in the evening a full-scale mutiny broke out.

The regiment's officers, none of whom had been sufficiently close to the men to have detected any change in their demeanour during the previous days, were taken completely by surprise. The remainder of the garrison, officers and men of the artillery, and of the commissariat and ordnance departments, were just as unprepared. Within a couple of hours the mutineers were in full control of the fort, and in the general confusion which had taken place seven officers had been killed. All the other white personnel, including a few women, had either been captured or had managed to escape in the darkness. It was not only the distant attitude of the regiment's officers which helped the mutineers; as was so often the case in any of the West India regiments, the number of officers actually serving was well below the authorised establishment. On this particular day there were only eleven officers in charge of almost five hundred men. Even the commanding officer was absent, "having gone to Europe, for the recovery of his health". Major John Gordon, who had assumed temporary command, was one of three who managed to escape and raise the alarm.

FACING PAGE
The plaque at Fort Shirley commemorates the Mutiny of 1802.

Ian Brierley / Hansib

Five of the others were amongst those killed, and the remaining three were held as hostages.

When news of the mutiny reached Roseau, the island's main town, the next morning, Johnstone declared martial law, mobilised the Militia, and called out the 68th Regiment from Morne Bruce just outside the town. As road communication on the island was so poor he requisitioned various small vessels in the roadstead, and these transported the troops and himself to Prince Rupert's Bay the same evening. The two warships, the *Excellent* and the *Magnificent*, which had only anchored in the bay the previous day to embark firewood and fresh water, were still there, and Johnstone found that their marines had already been landed in order to prevent anyone from leaving the fort. The *Magnificent* was despatched for reinforcements from among the troops occupying the Iles des Saintes off Guadeloupe, and when she returned on 12th April, Johnstone was able to muster a total of 1300 men. Preparations were then put in hand to storm the fort. Before this could take place the mutineers, using one of their hostages as a go-between, agreed to an unconditional surrender. Arrangements were made for Johnstone and his force to take over the fort at five o'clock in the afternoon, by which time the mutineers would be drawn up on parade where they would "lay down their arms, on receiving word from the governor".

The British troops, including a detachment of artillery, with Johnstone riding at their head, and followed by "all the civilians attached to the army ... anxious to be spectators of the approaching scene", entered the fort at the time agreed. They found the 8th West India Regiment in place on the parade ground, with "the three officers (their prisoners) standing in front of their respective companies, to the command of which, it appeared, they had been restored". At this point, instead of merely giving the order for their arms to be grounded, Johnstone felt called upon to make a speech and to chastise the regiment for disloyalty. His harangue, delivered from the saddle while backed by ranks of fully-armed white troops and several pieces of artillery, turned what should have

been a quick and painless operation into a bloodbath. Many of the mutineers could have had no understanding of what Johnstone was saying, and all of them must have been extremely tense and nervous. As their mumbles of discontent increased in volume Johnstone realised he had made a mistake, and "without losing further time, gave the word for them to order, and ground their arms". It was too late. Only a few men obeyed and when one of the others called out that "Governor Johnstone would cheat them", the British troops "scarcely waiting for orders, fired a volley". The three company commanders managed to escape unhurt but a least seventy of the men were killed or wounded. The remainder panicked; a few returned fire, killing or wounding a number of white soldiers, but the great majority attempted to flee from the parade ground. They were pursued through the fort and out to the end of the bluff, "from the top of which, two or three hundred of them precipitated themselves into the sea". Incredibly, very few were killed by their fall, and eventually all the others struggled ashore to be taken into custody. Some who managed to escape from the fort in the opposite direction avoided capture by hiding in the very swamps which Johnstone had been told to have cleared, but eventually all were hunted down by the Militia. By the time order was restored and all the regiment accounted for at least fifty had been killed and a similar number wounded.

Three days later, after Major Gordon had identified the ringleaders, seven soldiers were court-martialled, found guilty of "exciting and joining in mutiny" and sentenced to death. Soon afterwards they and the rest of the regiment were transported to Martinique, where the executions took place on 27th April. As it was still not clear to the army authorities why the mutiny had taken place a Court of Inquiry was convened at Fort Royal at the end of the month. The evidence obtained from the interrogation of Major Gordon and the other officers, and from some of the men, and which then formed part of the report sent to the Secretary of War, contained references to various irregularities in the way the men had been employed and paid. At the time of the mutiny none of the men had received the extra allowance they were entitled to, and most of them had not received their regular pay for several months. Although these facts were considered to be no more than incidental to the major cause of the mutiny – which was recognised as being the fear of the men of being sold as field slaves – they marked the beginning of the end for Johnstone.

On 24th May, by which time the 8th West India Regiment had been shipped to Barbados, another Court of Inquiry was convened, in order to investigate the state of the regimental accounts. The evidence that this unearthed of unusual and irregular transactions, involving both pay and rations for the troops, was enough to show that the actions of some of the officers, Johnstone in particular, had contributed much to the outbreak of the mutiny. This was confirmed in June, when another twenty-four men were court-martialled, and it was asserted "that short pay and want of money, were the general cry among the soldiers on the eve of the mutiny". All those tried, most bearing the foolish names they had had hung around their necks just a few years earlier – Mars, Congo Jack, Martyr, Manly, Lively – were found guilty and executed. Punishment of the rest of the regiment, now reduced to under four hundred, took place three months later. The one hundred and eighty-four men adjudged to have taken an active part in the mutiny were sent as pioneers to various white regiments where, no doubt, they were soon worked to death. The remainder, considered not to have been directly involved, were drafted into some of the other West India regiments. Although the 8th West India Regiment remained in being for another fourteen years, from September 1802 it consisted of officers and men of the 11th West India Regiment, which had been renumbered.

Out of the officers of the 'old' 8th West India Regiment who could be held culpable, only Johnstone and Gordon remained alive. Gordon was not given the opportunity of transferring into another regiment, but sent back to England on half-pay. Johnstone, who was dismissed from his post as governor of Dominica, lost his appointment as a brigadier and was put on half-pay as a colonel. He followed Gordon to England determined to revive his fortunes, and began by having Gordon arrested and court-martialled, charged with embezzlement, misuse of public funds and general dereliction of duty. The trial took place in London in February 1804, with Johnstone prosecuting. It lasted two weeks and involved the prosecutor and the accused in a series of charges and counter-charges, each trying to blame the other for what had taken place two years earlier. In the end, even though Gordon was acquitted on all charges, the officers who formed the court obviously reached their verdict with some reluctance. In finding him not guilty they recorded that he "procrastinated", showed "culpable neglect", was "very irregular, in not keeping an account of the monies which he received", and also "negligent, and to have subjected himself to censure, in not having taken further measures in order to have accounted for the whole of the monies which he had received". He remained on half-pay and was never employed again.

A year later, largely as a result of the accusations made by Gordon at his own trial, Johnstone himself was court-martialled for various "irregularities". Although he was eventually acquitted it brought his army career to an end. He was passed over for promotion to major-general and so resigned in order to try his luck elsewhere. In 1807, again through family influence and string-pulling, he secured a 'lucrative appointment' in Tortola. There he entered wholeheartedly into a new career of fraud, larceny and embezzlement, which he pursued both in the Caribbean and Great Britain for the next seven years. In 1814, he was the prime instigator of a plot to defraud the London Stock Exchange, in which he involved and ruined the reputation of his nephew, Admiral Thomas Cochrane, the tenth Earl of Dundonald. While awaiting trial for his part in the conspiracy Johnstone fled the country and disappeared from history. ∎

Extract taken from *The Empty Sleeve: The Story of the West India Regiments of the British Army* (Hansib, 1997)

From Colonialism to Independence

PHILBERT AARON

What have we, the Commonwealth of Dominica, achieved in the thirty years since Independence on 3rd November 1978? Who among us should Earl Etienne paint as icons? If our destiny is developed nation status, then, frankly, our report card is mixed. Our material culture – how many of our babies survive, how many persist how far in school, the burden of illness we bear, how many teeth we hold on to as we age, how many of us drive cars, at what age we die – has not much improved. Still, we rise in the morning to colourful rainbows.

Early on, we foiled a coup attempt and have since maintained a stable state. And in the process, we might just have strengthened the bonds of a post-colonial nation – the Kalinago, African, European, and Asian still get along. Moreover, we have forged this path in the face of natural and man-made disasters that might have decimated a less courageous people. Maybe that's not too bad for a nation whose foundations include genocide and slavery.

Thirty years after the Union Jack came down, I am proud to report that we are still a nation of laws. Our constitution is alive, our judiciary maintains its independence, we have an overactive legislative branch, a vibrant executive, and after pouring out into the streets to maintain a free press and the right to assemble and express our opinions freely just one year into our journey, we have five political parties and an active talk radio and overall media culture. Unemployment is high and per capita income is low. We still live by the sweat of our brows: most of us growing bananas or pulling tuna from the sea. Yes, some of us work in services, many serving visitors to the 'Nature Island of the Caribbean'. Fewer still work in manufacturing. Our motto, "Apres bondie c'est la ter," which means "After God, the earth," means so much more today than it did then. Our faith in the spirits and trust in nature have grown. These have been our humble achievements in the face of formidable odds; but the longest journey begins with one step.

Frustrated by our relative backwardness and recognising that Britain had been exhausted as an

PHOTO: EMEIL J. DEPOOTER JR

Irvin C. Durand

Patrick John (left) and Mary Eugenia Charles

inspiration, former Attorney General L.E.O. Austin provided the justification for a new flag, and for taking over our foreign affairs and the responsibility for our national security, and for more international development aid. Premier Patrick John championed the idea. Opposition Leader Mary Eugenia Charles expressed her reservations. Empowered by the democratic rule of numbers, John boldly cut our umbilical cord and started this journey, placing himself at the helm. Henceforth, we were on our own and proud of it.

But independence quickly proved to be a perilous journey. Still, all in the name of preserving law and order in Dominica, a motley crew of champions would form: a vigilant media, angry crowds, a sympathetic police force, and a Committee for National Salvation. The new head they chose, Oliver J. Seraphin, would rise to yet another challenge: 'David', our most devastating hurricane ever. And from that day on, hurricanes, clean-ups and the fate of politicians have been tightly bound. But the clean-up job that Dominica needed after the double-blow of constitutional crisis and tropical storm came in the form of Mary Eugenia Charles, the 'Iron Lady'. She would earn her time at the helm because of her fierce

(L-R) Oliver J. Seraphin, Roosevelt Douglas, Pierre Charles and Dominica's current Prime Minister, Roosevelt Skerrit.

commitment to decency in the management of the State.

The wheel kept on turning as it must and Edison James would earn his own time at the wheel by reminding us of the spirit animating our laws, freedom from fear and the coolness of his managerial expertise. By then, the robustness of the State itself would point radicals Roosevelt Douglas and Pierre Charles towards a milder path for putting the spotlight on the poor, use of the State's policy instruments for the cause of social justice. But no one would leverage the single most important legacy of political independence, the tool of independent foreign relations for national development as Dominica's current Prime Minister, Roosevelt Skerrit.

Today, we stand at a fork in the road. The vulnerabilities of a small island state go beyond the risk of hurricanes and constitutional crises. There are less visible but no less potent challenges. They include over exposure to outside international trade policy regimes, changes in economic trends overseas, and changes in technology. As a result, Dominica would face new pressures from the 1990s onwards. At the same time that hurricanes are ravaging the banana industry locally, deep changes

in ways of doing business internationally are disrupting overseas markets for Dominica's green gold. Haitian migrants would fill in the void left by nationals who are finding the conditions of agricultural labour increasingly unattractive. Yet, new forms of work in the tourist industry, call centres, and in agricultural processing, cannot keep pace.

In the face of incredible odds, a number of actors go to work, fortifying the nation from many fields. Gordon Henderson, Midnight Groovers, and Ophelia in Cadence Lypso and De Ency, Scrunter, Hunter, Dice, Pat Aaron and Swinging Stars in calypso provide the soundtrack for a nation's struggles for survival and decency. Lennox Honychurch continues to serve as the librarian of our long-term memory while *The Chronicle*, *The Sun*, DBS Radio, Q95 FM & Kairi FM radio and our local talk show hosts keep jogging our short-term memory. Bernard Wiltshire and Artherton Martin, among others in the environmental movement, struggle to define Dominica by its naturalness. Those are some faces who will be sculpted, painted, sung, and impressed upon postage stamps. Yet, the question that begs answering is: Are the beautiful ones who will take Dominica to the Promised Land already born? ∎

Roseau is the central media hub
Photo: Irvin C. Durand

A century of media development

ALEX BRUNO

Dominica's media is on the verge of a major accomplishment with the *Chronicle* newspaper celebrating its centenary in January 2009. The newspaper is also one of the Caribbean's oldest publications and is therefore the undisputed 'Queen' of the Dominica media.

The media is a unique institution which operates not just as 'media', but rather as a catalyst for growth and nation building. The involvement of the media in all aspects of our social endeavours is easily traced to the pre-colonial era. However, a new sense of purpose was realised when in 1967 the country attained Associated Statehood under the then Chief Minister, Edward Oliver LeBlanc. It was LeBlanc who began the process to nationalise vital institutions including the media, which was then empowered with the responsibility of supporting and promoting cultural diversity and national pride.

LeBlanc's momentum led the nation to independence on 3rd November 1978 under Prime Minister, Patrick John, and as we look back to thirty years, there are many shining examples of media driven success. Since independence, a string of institutions has been created along the way; cadence music was created; co-operatives became a buzzword; a proud National Bank was born; cultural practices and awareness peaked; learning was made easier; doors of opportunity were opened with the new enlightenment by the media; the world

as we knew it became smaller; the richness of the Nature Island was realised; our music became 'king' on other shores and the World Creole Music Festival was created.

For all of these to have been accomplished, there was the necessity for the prerequisite media foundation work. The establishment of Radio Dominica on 1st November 1971 replaced the Windward Island Broadcasting Services (WIBS) and complemented the British Broadcasting Corporation (BBC) and Voice of America. This new wave ignited a media fire which has been kept burning by a procession of broadcasters and institutions.

The local media has witnessed and reported on all of the national developments. It ushered in the new waves of political leaders and their parties: the Dominica United People's Party (DUPP), Dominica Labour Party (DLP), Dominica Interim

Government, Dominica Freedom Party (DFP), United Workers Party (UWP) and then back to the DLP. The media has been there through all the political administrations, with breaking news, reporting and commentary.

The media has also witnessed and reported on the government-toppling uprisings of the 1970s; the Dread Act era; countless corruption charges; the mud-slinging during General Elections; the discrimination against individuals; tragedies; executions; the Carnival fire of 1963; the burning of the Registry; and the deaths of three prime ministers and one head of government between 2000 and 2005. On numerous occasions, the media was also forced to defend itself.

The media in Dominica operates in a non-conventional way and, as such, the nation is the better for it. ■

Icons of the Nation

A PERSONAL ASSESSMENT BY DR PHILBERT AARON

The Mount Rushmore National Memorial in the United States is renowned for the faces of four presidents that are carved into it: George Washington, Thomas Jefferson, Theodore Roosevelt and Abraham Lincoln. Those four presidents, who represent the first 150 years of history of the US, are icons. But Gutzon Borglum, the lead sculptor of the monument, is clear about what is carved into that mass of granite. It is neither moonlight scene nor tragedy, he wrote, but something constructive, a contribution to civilisation. Lofty stuff indeed; mythic.

Every nation needs a few myths. In Dominica, there are two groups of myths: One relates to the land, the other relates to its people. Within the first set is the myth of Edenic Dominica, uniquely blessed with water, sunshine and greenery. Forming a counterpoint to Eden is Dominica the cursed: tiny with forbidding mountains and in the path of hurricanes. Within the second is the myth that Dominicans are pure of heart and race. Its counterpoint is that Dominicans are related to sharks: fractious, ungovernable. In short, a storyline that is triumphant, with a leader as its hero, is yet to emerge. But every nation needs a storyline. Why? Because it is that storyline, real or imagined, that generates the country's development plan – the value, vision, mission and objectives. Still, most accounts of our history parade all our leaders without distinction. I, however, believe that it is time to sculpt our own Mount Rushmore. To begin the debate I propose a unifying myth. I propose the myth of the resilient Dominica. When we get knocked down, be it by hurricane or man-made folly, we get up again. And that, I propose, is the defining quality, above all else, of Dominica.

Three of our prime ministers embody that resiliency above all others. They are E.O. LeBlanc, Mary Eugenia Charles and our present Prime Minister, Roosevelt Skerrit. In the work of all three, the nation was stretched to lengths that helped it to survive. LeBlanc pulled us out of colonial backwardness and set us on a path forward into independence. Charles led us out of the physical and political chaos in the aftermath of Hurricane David

and the May 29 Revolt. And Skerrit is providing a steady hand in the wake of the demise of promising predecessors and a near-catastrophic fiscal crisis. So here is my justification for whom I would propose for Dominica's version of Mount Rushmore.

EDWARD OLIVER LEBLANC

Dominica's first premier, Edward Oliver LeBlanc, has the status of America's George Washington, and with good reason. His struggle was to modernise Dominica in realms both political and economic. And he saw the two linked in the 'barefoot man', whom he saw as a legacy of our long and shameful colonial past and rose up against it. He addressed the psychology of the little man in Dominica by rehabilitating his culture, especially his dances and his language. And he tackled the material poverty of the little man by hacking away at the land tenure system as well as providing geographic access through infrastructure projects.

LeBlanc is arguably the most revered political figure in our history, winning a seat for himself in district after district and weathering the storms of political infighting and ultimately working his way back to the top. Today, Dominica is so much better off because of E.O. LeBlanc. He placed the little man on the political map and set us on the course towards ultimate freedom and independence.

MARY EUGENIA CHARLES

The Caribbean's first female prime minister, Mary Eugenia Charles has the reputation for being Dominica's 'Iron Lady', a title that is derived from Britain's Iron Lady, Margaret Thatcher, but the comparison is a disservice to Dame Eugenia. Eugenia Charles means much more as both a woman and a leader. For one, she was an independent woman. That sets her apart from the women who rose to prominence because they

BELOW
Eugenia Charles is arguably the second most successful politician in Dominica's history.

PHOTO COURTESY PRIME MINISTER'S OFFICE

RIGHT
A visit by Prime Minister Roosevelt Skerrit draws an admiring crowd of schoolchildren in San Sauveur.

were the wives or daughters of prominent men. Yes, Eugenia was the daughter of a powerful man but she constructed her public career rather independently, eclipsing her father by every measure possible. Eugenia Charles is arguably the second most successful politician in Dominica's history, serving as party leader and prime minister for three consecutive terms. And what did she contribute? Charles is possibly our most cerebral leader to date. She raised the stakes on the old Labour Party, focusing less on politics and more on policy. And in the realm of policy, hers was an emphasis on ideas and ideals, especially those that were related to decency in the management of the state. Eugenia Charles embodied decency in state affairs in the symbolic realm in her personal manner, in her bearing, her language, as well as in the substantial areas of public governance. She turned her political fortunes around from being a long-time Opposition figure to making a smooth transition to office. And in office, she wrestled with the weightiest questions of the day: What price liberty? What price material progress? The crises of Hurricane David and the uprisings of 29 May 1979, that had left our economy and our democracy in a near-death state, were the barriers she had to overcome to lead Dominica. She tackled both with gusto, and in so doing, Mary Eugenia Charles has sculpted her own place into Dominica's historical landscape.

ROOSEVELT SKERRIT

Prime Minister Roosevelt Skerrit has rock star status, but that masks the depth of the leader in him. He is more the spiritual heir of E.O. LeBlanc both in leadership style and in philosophy. Skerrit has received the baton from LeBlanc and is off in the struggle for decency of the barefoot man. Skerrit's commitment to equity within as well as between nations is the unifying focus of his leadership. Foreign relations are the single most important tools of our nationhood, and no other leader in the history of Dominica has utilised it as skilfully as Skerrit. I say skilfully because, guided by the principle that foreign policy is driven by domestic priorities, he has constantly kept his eyes on the prize: Dominica's development.

Pierre Charles charted a course out of our recent fiscal crisis and Skerrit has stayed that course. He has established profitable partnerships with China and Venezuela, joining the ALBA, the Bolivarian Alternative for Latin America and the Caribbean when the benefits were clear to only a few. And he has delivered to Dominica half of our national dream: a national stadium (an international jet airport is the other half). And although Skerrit is the spiritual heir of E.O. LeBlanc, he has the focus and incisive grasp of the big issues of the day that Mary Eugenia Charles showed in public life. ■

Celebrating the women of Dominica

MARCELLA LAROCQUE-MENAL

The Dominican woman is a virtuous woman, a remarkable woman. Her life mirrors that of a noble woman. She is a strong, multi-talented, dignified and caring woman, who is an individual in her own right. A parallel with the ideal woman as illustrated in Proverbs 31 is made with some of Dominica's best.

"In her hands she holds the distaff and grasps the spindle with her fingers" (vs. 19). Dominica's musical landscape has been greatly enhanced by the skills and talents of contributors like Pearle Christian, Sonia Lloyd, Yuguette Andrew-St Hilaire, Mayma Joseph and Valena Letang. The grand dame of our folkloric fabric, Mabel "Cissy" Caudeiron, served as a cultural activist, a Creole nationalist whose tool for nation-building was folk traditions, especially Creole songs. The accomplishments of Jean Lawrence-Mathurin continue to resonate with the uniqueness of our culture and a nostalgia that embraces Dominicans worldwide. Our Lady of Song, Ophelia, possesses a personality that can pervade the atmosphere of an entire concert hall with her infectious rhythms. These reins are now

being shared with Michelle Henderson, whose musical career, though relatively young, has blossomed with strong international appeal.

Dominica's literary tapestry has been woven by a varied collection of talented writers, the most notable being Jean Rhys, who is the most internationally recognised female author from the Caribbean. Phyllis Shand Allfrey's *The Orchid House* is a prominent Caribbean work and is featured in most articles on West Indian literature and was also made into a film. Today, we turn the pages penned by some of our modern-day writers like Dr Kay Polydore, Ivenia Benjamin, Dorothy Leevy and Gloria Augustus who hone their skills through application.

"Her lamp does not go out at night" (vs. 18) because as a good steward she takes pride in her work. The women's contribution to politics in Dominica has left an indelible mark. Dame Mary Eugenia Charles had the distinction of being Dominica's first female lawyer and Prime Minister. She earned herself the title, 'Iron Lady of the Caribbean' due mainly to her unflinching dedication

FACING PAGE
Dominica State College. Education is a vital cornerstone in the lives of many Dominican women.
Irvin C. Durand

RIGHT
Enterprising women ply their trade throughout the land, both in the selling and production of goods.
Ian Brierley / Hansib

and unyielding will to set principles, based on her beliefs. More women shone in the political sphere as Speaker of the House: Marie Davis-Pierre, Neva Edwards and currently Alix Boyd-Knights; and as Minister of Government: Gertrude Roberts, Vernice Bellony and Hon. Loreen Bannis-Roberts. Of worthy note is Dominican-born the Rt. Hon. Baroness Patricia Scotland who is Britain's first Black Attorney General and the first female to hold the position.

The enterprising Dominican woman is one who "considers a field and buys it; from her earnings she plants a vineyard" (vs. 16). In the field of business, a generous helping of respect must be paid to Vena McDougall of Vena's Guesthouse; Janice Armour of the Anchorage Hotel; Annette St Hilaire of Continental Store; and Lucia Stedman, who helps build our human resource capacity at her Business Training Centre. The trail of the businesswoman can be seen throughout Dominica as they remain the forefront grocer, snackette-owner or roadside stall vendor, such as Miranda's Corner at Springfield. Our agricultural heritage continues to thrive primarily because of the care and grace given by women through the traditions of field cultivation, particularly in banana production, where we celebrate icons such as Bella Joachim. Today, over half of our hucksters, who venture beyond our shores to trade and feed our northern neighbours, are women of valour.

"She opens her mouth in wisdom, and the teaching of kindness is on her tongue" (vs. 26). Devoted Educators like Celia Nicholas, Rose Johnson "Brown Owl", Josephine Joseph, Josephine Dublin, and Edith Bellot have all shaped the minds of those entrusted to their care. Their love for children and dedication to task is demonstrated in the humane service that they give. Hatty Leslie, Isabella Prentice, Patsy Emmanuel, Glenda Betrand, Cyrilla Anselm and Josette Matthew can almost be considered adopted mothers to the children they teach.

"She girds herself with strength, and makes her arms strong" (vs. 17). In February 2005, Dominica was home to twenty-one centenarians, the majority being women, with the oldest at the age of 107. Elizabeth "Ma Pampo" Israel, whom Dominicans believe was the oldest living person at age 128, attributed her longevity to her diet: callaloo, crab, cane sugar, fish, bush tea and lots of dumplings. Alex Bruno, local centenarian activist, recalls from his many conversations with these gems that the majority sees old age as a blessing from God, and believes that they live long because of their simplicity, virtue and honesty. These centenarians, when encountered, are excellent raconteurs, who have a varied stock of stories; their voices affectionate, never spoiling the stories with a heavy-handed moral.

The culinary heritage of Dominica, as embraced by our centenarians, is not lost, since today some of our seasoned caterers and culinary experts serve a delightful array of local delicacies prepared not only with the best of local herbs, fruits, ground provisions and spices, but with much passion. These subtle combinations excite the most aloof palettes. When Nathalie Charles, known for her vegetarian cuisine, Joan Cools-Lartigue (Orchard Restaurant), Hermina Astaphan (Guiyave), Pearle Pinnard (Pearle's Cuisine), Joan Maynard, Fae Martin, Elenore Lambert (nutritionist), Alison Southwell, Erica Burnette-Biscombe (La Robe Creole), Nurse Symes and her daughter Dawn, Delia Grell, Justina James, and Alix Boyd-Knights, work their magic in those sacred kitchens, those who are fortunate enough to be present are faced with a Hobson's choice: indulge in the savoury treats, or eat nothing at all!

Who is a virtuous woman today? Proverbs 31 tells that it is the woman who puts God first. This ideal woman should encourage women everywhere. Cultures change, but this woman's God-inspired character still shines brightly across the centuries. Anyone wishing to encounter a virtuous woman needs only meet a Dominican woman and "Give her the product of her hands, and let her works praise in the gates" (vs. 31). ■

FACING PAGE
Anyone wishing to encounter a virtuous woman needs only meet a Dominican woman.

RIGHT
The trail of the businesswoman can be seen throughout Dominica as they remain the forefront grocer, snackette-owner or roadside stall vendor.

Photos: Ian Brierley

Post Independence sporting achievements

OSWALD SAVARIN

It may come as a surprise to some, but Dominica has experienced significant development in sport during the post Independence period. Most of our major sporting achievements occurred during this time, which can be described as a period of restructuring and expanded sporting programmes and services.

In the area of restructuring, there were two important developments. The first was the establishment of the Sports Division in 1980, and years later in 1993, the formal recognition of the Dominica Olympic Committee (DOC) by the International Olympic Committee (IOC).

The initiative which resulted in the formation of the DOC and its subsequent affiliation to the IOC, had inspired a number of national sports associations to become affiliated to their respective international federation. Currently there are sixteen National Sports Associations affiliated to the DOC and their respective International Federations. These include athletics, archery, basketball, boxing, bodybuilding, bridge, cricket, football, lawn tennis, netball, rifle, squash, swimming, table tennis, taekwon-do and volleyball.

Dominica's first appearance at the Summer Olympics in 1996 in Atlanta was a major accomplishment for sport in Dominica. The team of six athletes, comprising Jerome Romain, Dawn Williams-Sewer, Hermine Joseph, Cedric Harris, Stephen Agar and Woodrow Lawrence, participated in a wide range of track and field events and swimming.

Despite not having attained an Olympic medal, Dominica received worldwide attention when Jerome Romain, achieved a bronze medal in the triple jump at the World Athletics Championships held in Gothenburg, Sweden in 1995. Earlier that year in Argentina, Jerome had given an indication of his triple jumping prowess when he secured the silver medal during the Pan American Games. Besides Jerome, several other Track and Field athletes have earned medals at regional and international Games. The most recent outstanding performers were Chris Lloyd, who won silver in the 400m event at 2007 PanAm Games, and Tyrone

Benjamin who won a silver medal in the shot put event at the same Games. Dominica has also produced several Carifta Games medallists including gold medallist Lisa Casimir, Dawn Williams-Sewer, Jerome Romain and most recently Dillon Simon in the Under-17 shot put in 2007.

Jerome Romain is by far the most accomplished track and field athlete Dominica has ever produced. In cricket, however, Dominica can boast of several outstanding players. Most notable is Irving Shillingford who, together with Norbert Phillip, Grayson Shillingford and Adam Sanford remain our only test cricketers. Irving's 120 runs against Pakistan in 1978 is worthy of mention because it demonstrated Irving's class and vindicated the many who thought that Irving was unlucky not to have been selected on the West Indies team earlier in his career.

Dominica's cricket was probably at its best prior to Independence. Irving still played in the early eighties but other great players were making their mark in the 1980s and 1990s, enabling Dominica to win the Windward Islands Cricket Tournament nine times consecutively from 1981 to 1990. Some of the key players of that era included Norbert Phillip, who took over the captaincy from Irving Shillingford, Lockhart Sebastien, Thomas Kentish, Jevan Ettienne, Roy Marshall and Joey Pierre. Lockhart Sebastien who retired from the game in 1990 still holds the record for the most runs in Windward Islands Cricket. After 1990, Dominica's wins became less frequent and gradually, Dominica lost its dominance of Windward Islands cricket. Other sports had their moments of glory during the period under review but never attained a level of dominance close to that of cricket.

There were, however, Windward Islands Championship titles for the national senior football team in 1985 and 1990. Basketball also did well during the years of regular OECS basketball competitions, winning three OECS Championship titles. In addition, the association under the leadership of Mickey Joseph was very instrumental in securing United States scholarships for its top players. To date, about eight Dominicans have

FACING PAGE
Towering above the girls' basketball team, Garth Joseph is the first and only Dominican to play in the NBA. He also has the distinction of being Dominica's tallest person.

Ian Brierley / Hansib

Practice session by the Dominica cricket team at Windsor Park Stadium. Officially opened in 2007, the stadium has already hosted regional cricket and football matches and plans are underway for Dominica's hosting of its first international cricket match.

Ian Brierley / Hansib

benefited from this initiative. The first to receive a basketball scholarship after Independence was Garth Joseph who in 1995 became the first and only Dominican to play in the NBA. Garth Joseph is currently a professional basketball player.

Volleyball is another sport which made steady progress in the OECS region. The national senior men's team, after holding the second place position behind St Lucia for a number of years, was finally able to raise its game in 2000 to win the OECS Men's Volleyball Championship. Dominica followed this up by winning the OECS Female Championship title in 2001. Dominica became Champions again in 2006 (Women) and 2007 (Men).

Boxing grew in popularity during the last fifteen years as the Association strengthened its organisation and provided increased opportunities for local boxers to receive training and participate in several boxing championships. The best result obtained by our national boxers occurred in 2007 when Dominica won the OECS boxing championship title.

In netball, while our senior national team struggled, our top shooter, Jennifer Nanton, stood out as one of the Caribbean's top players. She represented Dominica from 1982 to 2001 and

performed consistently at a high level during her long period of national service. She was one of three Dominicans who, during the 1990s, were selected on a West Indies training squad. The other two were Marvella Germain and Frances Morancie. Marvella Germain who was multi-talented secured a basketball scholarship to the USA but later changed to volleyball.

Table tennis, regarded by many to be a minority sport, made tremendous strides during the 1980s and 1990s. Anthony Dailey (deceased) was a tough young player who was difficult to beat. In 1989, he won the OECS top 20 singles championship title. Dominica then went on to win the OECS men's team title in 1992 with players Brian Matthew, Brett Stephens, Donald Corriette and Samuel Dailey. This was Dominica's first OECS table tennis team title. In 1996 and 1997, Dominica won back-to-back OECS Table Tennis Championship titles in both team and singles events. Dominica last won the Championship title in 2002.

Bridge, too, had its fair share of glory winning OECS titles in 1989, 1990 and 2000. The Dominica teams showed their dominance of the OECS Championship when they won consecutive titles in 2005, 2006 and 2007. Dominica also played tournaments on a regular basis against Martinique and after fourteen tournaments, Dominica emerged champions about ten times.

Before Independence, opportunities for Dominica's youth to participate in regional competitions were few. Throughout the eighties to the present, these opportunities increased to include cricket at U-13, U-15 and U-20 (Gary Sobers), netball at U-13, U-16 and U-23, football at U-15, U-17 and U-20. New sports were added to the Windward Islands School Games providing even more opportunities for our youth to participate in regional tournaments. The new sports included netball, volleyball and basketball. Table tennis had a brief appearance at the Games during the late 1980s. The performance of several of Dominica's youth teams remained strong even during the lean period experienced by some of our national senior teams.

Our team to the Sir Garfield Sobers Cricket Tournament won the tournament three times and reached the finals on four occasions. Dominica first participated in 1996. Between 1996 and 2004 Dominica won the U-19 Cricket tournament five times. The national U-15 cricket team was similarly successful and made history when it captured the Windward Islands U-15 Cricket Championship title twice in 2006 and again in 2007. Dominica's leading U-15 player, Kavem Hodge, then went on to captain

LEFT
During the 1980s and early 1990s, a programme of hard-court facility construction assisted the development of basketball.
Ian Brierley / Hansib

The current Dominica cricket squad hopes to emulate the successes of the teams of the 1980s.

Ian Brierley / Hansib

the Windward Islands U-15 cricket team to its first West Indies U-15 Cricket Championship title in 2007.

Our U-13 cricketers also achieved a great victory in 2008 when they became the first Dominican team in any sport to defeat both Barbados and Trinidad and Tobago to win a championship title. The U-13 cricket team, after placing third in the twenty-five overs a-side competition, bounced back to win the 10 overs a-side knockout competition.

Other successes by our youth teams include Dominica's Windward Islands Schools Games victories in 1998, 1999 and 2001. This represented the strongest showing by Dominica at these Games. Dominica's last win at the Games was in 2007 when Dominica emerged joint champions with Grenada.

Government's support for sport in general and for Dominica's participation in regional and international tournaments at both youth and senior levels have been in the form of grants, tax exemptions and facility development. In 1993, the Dominica Lotteries Commission came into being and has over the years provided funding for numerous sports projects inclusive of travel grants for national association teams.

Facility development was another area which received Government's attention during the post-Independence period. During the 1980s and early 1990s, a programme of hard-court facility construction assisted the development of basketball and, to a lesser extent, netball and volleyball. More recently, major playing field developments have led to the decentralisation of cricket and football, in the same manner as the hard courts assisted in spreading the sport of basketball island-wide.

Of significance are the Lio Park Playing Field in Marigot, the RMG Grounds at La Plaine, the Geneva Playing Field and the Benjamin's Park in Portsmouth. As a result, these facilities have become important venues for hosting local league matches. In addition, the transformation of the Benjamin's Park and the Geneva Playing Field have provided Dominica with acceptable alternatives to the Botanic Gardens and the Windsor Park for the hosting of regional cricket and football matches.

The Windsor Park is today the site of Dominica's first international sports stadium. This facility, which was officially opened in 2007, is by far Dominica's greatest achievement in sports development. This multi million-dollar gift from the People's Republic of China has already hosted regional cricket and football matches and plans are underway for Dominica's hosting of its first international cricket match in the near future.

As we look towards the next thirty years, it is incumbent on all concerned to work together to build on our successes and learn from our failures. It is not too early for the DOC and the relevant national associations to begin preparations for the 2012 Olympic Games. In this regard, Government, through the Sports Division, has already approached the DOC in informal discussions with the view of bringing all stakeholders together to assist Dominica raise its profile at the next Olympic Games. ■

Nature Island of the Caribbean

ARLINGTON JAMES

Dominica is popularly referred to as the 'Nature Island of the Caribbean', not only for her towering mountains, crystal clear streams, stunning coastal scenery, tumbling waterfalls, steaming fumaroles and "soufrieres", but also for the richness and diversity of her plant and animal life. In fact, it is this unique mix of gifts from Mother Nature that sets Dominica apart from the rest of the Eastern Caribbean, where it stands second to none in terms of its biological diversity and its eco-tourism potential.

The island's rugged topography, with mountains towering above 4,000 ft, has resulted in an incredibly high rainfall – up to 350 inches in the interior – as well as a wide variety of vegetation types. These include windswept littoral woodland with its 'trimmed-hedge' appearance hugging the windward coast; dry forest, scrub woodland and savannah-type vegetation (with clumps of cacti clinging to overhanging rocks) on and near the leeward coast; and small scattered patches of swamps and marshes in coastal and highland areas.

Venture into the island's jagged interior and climb one of the mountains, and you will encounter some of the most impressive examples of tropical rainforest in the wider Caribbean, as well as dripping, moss-covered trees and other plants in the montane forest. And while still spellbound by such sheer natural appeal, you may venture to clamber over the tops of kaklen trees in the elfin woodland near the summit of our taller mountains.

The fumarole vegetation growing at Wotten Waven, Valley of Desolation and near the Boiling Lake, at Galleon and Soufriere Sulphur Springs in the south, and the Cold Soufriere in the north, has somehow defied mankind's simple understanding of what is required for plants to grow and develop. These plants have adapted to a harsh sulphur-based environment, thereby adding to our rich botanical diversity.

Most of the species of wild plants and animals which occur on Dominica also exist in several other areas in the tropical world. However, there are a number of species found here that occur only in

FACING PAGE
The stark contrast between red and green in the ginger lily is mirrored in many plants throughout the island.

RIGHT
A banana quit finds sustenance from the nuni fruit.

Photos: Ian Brierley

LEFT
Dominica is home to many striking examples of flowering plants.
Ian Brierley / Hansib

the Lesser Antilles, and fewer still that occur only on Dominica. These species are referred to as being endemic to the Lesser Antilles (regional endemics), or Dominican endemic species accordingly, and will not be found in the wild anywhere else in the world.

Dominica's best-known endemic plant is our National Flower, "Bwa Kwaib" (*Sabinea carinalis*), which officially became a national emblem in 1978. The plant grows in the dry scrubby vegetation along the island's leeward coast, between Loubiere and Capuchin. It is deciduous and showy, and for a few weeks during every dry season (February to June), bwa kwaib will shed its leaves, and its slender branches will be covered by masses of scarlet flowers.

Another of Dominica's endemic plants is *Pitcairnia micotrinensis*, a member of the pineapple family; it is called "zannanna flè jòn" on account of its light yellow flowers. This terrestrial bromeliad is one of the dominant plants in the Valley of Desolation and near Boiling Lake. The plants, with their inflorescences and slender dark green leaves, set against a backdrop of coloured streams, hissing fumaroles and bubbling pools of hot grey mud, seemingly defying nature, more often than not catch the attention of not only the naturalists but casual hikers alike journeying to and from the world's second-largest, thermally-active lake.

The buttressed and/or sometimes stilt-rooted "Karapit" or "Break-Nail" (*Amanoa caribaea*) abounds in our rainforest. This is a much-prized species as it is endemic only to Guadeloupe and Dominica. It is a very important tree for our two species of parrot which feed on its fruits and use its cavities for nesting. The "Yataw" or "Kokoyé" – one of the native palms from the northern half of the island – is endemic only to the islands from Montserrat to St Lucia, while yet another palm *Aiphanes minima* ("Gwigwi" and "Gouglou zonbi") with its long thorns, is also endemic to the Lesser Antilles.

LEFT & FACING PAGE
The lesser Antillean iguana, as its name suggests, is restricted to a few Lesser Antillean islands. By far the largest population of this iguana exists on Dominica.
Photos: Ian Brierley

CLOCKWISE FROM TOP
Bwa Kwaib grows in the dry scrubby vegetation along the island's leeward coast and is Dominica's national flower.
Photo: Irvin C. Durand

Crustaceans and reptiles live cheek by jowl but not always in harmony; this crab preys on iguana hatchlings.
Photo: Ian Brierley

Dominica has 55 species of butterfly, of which three are endemic to the island.
Photo: Ian Brierley

Adding to the island's rich plant diversity are about 188 species of fern and 70-80 species of orchid – including four species of vanilla, the endemic *Epidendrum discoidale*, and David's orchid (*Spathoglotis plicata*) which is reputed to have involuntarily arrived here on the winds of the mighty Hurricane David in 1979.

Dominica has other endemic plants, such as *Eugenia hodgei*, *Miconia mornicola* and *Inga dominicensis*, but these are found in remote places such as the elfin woodlands near some of Dominica's mountain tops.

Among the Nature Island's impressive assemblage of wild fauna – which has been described as "the most diverse" in the Eastern Caribbean – are several species that are endemic only to Dominica, and several other Lesser Antillean endemics. These include frogs, birds, lizards, three butterflies, a species of bat, and even stick insects.

In the 1990s, one of our three species of frog *Eleutherodactylus amplinympha* was confirmed as endemic for Dominica. This little frog, whose females are much larger than the males, inhabits areas that are 2,500 ft above sea level in the Morne Trois Pitons National Park, the Morne Diablotin National Park and the Northern Forest Reserve. What may just be for us in Dominica our former National Dish, the "Mountain Chicken" (*Leptodactylus fallax*) – the world's second largest species of frog – could once be found in the forested islands from St Lucia to St Kitts; this frog now inhabits only Montserrat and Dominica, and

FACING PAGE
Indian River is a popular boating location and gives visitors the chance to see nature at close quarters.
Ian Brierley / Hansib

LEFT
The red anthurium is a popular addition to bouquets and flower arrangements.
Photo: Irvin C. Durand

LEFT
An array of colours can be seen amid the sea of green leaves.

FAR LEFT
The "Zanndoli" or tree lizard is one of ten species of lizard that are native to Dominica.
Photos: Ian Brierley

is now threatened with extinction here by the chytrid fungus. Our other frog, the well-known "gounouj", is endemic to the Lesser Antilles.

Our National Bird, the Sisserou parrot (*Amazona imperialis*) and the smaller but more abundant Jaco parrot (*Amazona arausiaca*) are also endemic only to the Nature Island. In fact, Dominica is somewhat special in terms of our bird life, in that we are the only small island in the world with two endemic species of Amazon parrots. Thirteen other regional endemics from the Lesser Antilles also occur on Dominica. These include the Blue-headed hummingbird which is endemic only to Dominica and Martinique, and the Plumebous warbler (*Dendroica petechia*) which occurs only on Guadeloupe, Marie Galante and Dominica. Some of our other regionally endemic birds include the Antillean euphonia, Lesser Antillean bullfinch, the Antillean-crested, Purple-throated and Green-throated hummingbirds, among other birds.

Ten native species of lizard occur here, including the "Zanndoli" or tree lizard (*Anolis oculatus*) – which exhibits an impressive variety of colour patterns – and the Abòlò (*Ameiva fuscata*). These two lizards are Dominican endemics. The "Léza" (*Iguana delicatissima*), or Lesser Antillean iguana as its name suggests, is restricted to a few Lesser Antillean islands. By far the largest population of this iguana

FACING PAGE
The hibiscus is a common sight throughout Dominica.

Ian Brierley / Hansib

FACING PAGE
The Botanical Gardens in Roseau provide the perfect opportunity to see a wide variety of plants and flowers like this 'powder puff'.

RIGHT
Hummingbirds are a delicate and graceful feature of the Nature Island of the Caribbean.
Photos: Ian Brierley

exists on Dominica. With the exception of La Desirade and one of The Saints in the French Department of Guadeloupe, the species has virtually disappeared from the other islands.

Dominica is also home to four confirmed species of snake, viz. the Boa constrictor, "Kouwès jenga", "Kouwes nwè" and "Koulèv" (none venomous); all are species or sub-species that are locally endemic.

Three of our eleven species of stick insect or "Chouval Bwa", three of the 55 species of butterfly (Dominican hairstreak, Dominican snout and Godman's leaf), and at least two of our 36 species of snail, and two of the 21 species of dragonfly and damselfly are endemic to the Nature Island. On an island where nature abounds, one can expect the list of endemic species to be impressive, and to include moths, some of the 24 species of mosquito, centipedes, spiders and other invertebrate creatures.

Thus, while the Caribbean has been labelled as one of the world's "biodiversity hotspots" with an outstanding list of endemic fauna and flora, Dominica, irrespective of its small size contributes in an impressive way to this master list, in terms of our plants, birds, snakes, lizards, frogs, bats, various insects and other invertebrates that can all be labelled "uniquely Dominican". It is precisely because of such natural endowment that, to date, three national parks (including a World Heritage Site) have been established to preserve part of the habitat for some of these species. There are, however, a number of other endemic species that are not found in any of our protected areas. Therefore, the time may be right for us as Dominicans to begin that journey together and so discover or rediscover other such natural attributes, and so put the necessary measures in place to ensure that we preserve all of our endemic species. Together they make up one of the essential elements that undoubtedly contribute to our Nature Island image. ∎

Diving in an underwater park

A PERSONAL JOURNEY BY SIMON WALSH

For the many people who might not be familiar with the experience of taking a dive excursion, I would like to take you on a dive in our underwater world. While we are taking this imaginary dive, let us celebrate the journey together by showing what makes Dominica such an extraordinary experience for all those who dive here.

The fist step is to choose one of the nine dive shops on the west coast. All of these establishments are members of the Dominica Watersports Association (DWA) and are registered and inspected by the Department of Fisheries. The DWA has been instrumental in setting the region's highest safety standards, establishing marine reserves and for providing local educational programmes for employment in the industry. So, whichever dive shop you choose, you can expect to dive with a well-trained dive master who is familiar with all the sites and their attractions.

Once certification has been verified, the dive boat sets off for the desired location. The journey may be as short as ten minutes but in no time at all the dive master will be tying the boat up to a mooring. These moorings were installed through a joint effort between the DWA and the Department of Fisheries, with funding from the European Union (EU). This united commitment ensures that the reefs are protected for future generations.

With the boat safely moored, it's time for the dive briefing. The purpose of this is to review the safety procedures and to ensure that each participant understands how the dive will be conducted. During this briefing, the dive master will also outline the key aspects of the dive site and describe the topography and marine life that will be encountered.

The divers are now ready to take the first plunge into the crystal clear waters. As the bubbles begin to clear, and the divers get their bearings, it soon becomes evident why Dominica is consistently rated as one of the world's leading dive locations. Because of the clean waters, the reefs are healthy; marine life is abundant, colourful and thriving.

The dive master will now signal his charges to follow as he begins the tour. As you glide along the reef, you will witness fishes of all shapes and colours, corals and sponges, and plant life gently waving in the current. As the reef drops away into the dark blue abyss you feel strangely airborne as you stare into the depths 1500 feet below.

A hawksbill turtle swims beneath you, turning slightly to inspect the strange visitor. You resist the temptation to reach out and touch this beautiful creature. Then a larger green turtle passes you by on its way to the surface for a breath of fresh air. The dive master points into the blue yonder and then holds his arms outstretched, and then you spot the barracuda gently cruising by. This dive just keeps getting better. But like all good things, it must come to an end … but let's do it again!

Dominica truly has one of the Caribbean's most pristine and vibrant reefs offering a world-class dive experience. It is up to all of us to ensure that years from now, others will be extolling the virtues of Dominica's spectacular Marine Reserve.

Dominica's reefs are healthy and marine life is abundant, colourful and thriving.
Photos: Simon Walsh

Tourism in Dominica: The natural choice

CARLA ARMOUR

Dominica is wild, untameable and beautiful with a verdant landscape like a soft green rug strewn crumpled in opposition to the tranquil Caribbean Sea.

With oars suspended and sails billowing, the Kalinago's ancestors gasped, "Wai'tukubuli!" Dominica was so named, 'Tall is her body' by these early Caribbean settlers whose descendants still inhabit the island. Centuries later, Africans would traverse the island's secret spaces for refuge, communing in nature's bounty for decades while traders from Europe would drop anchor in the sheltered coves to restock their wood and water supplies. In spite of Dominica's fierce resistance to colonisation, visitors and settlers have arrived here for centuries, mostly for the same reasons: for shelter, sustenance, rest and inspiration.

Long before 'eco-tourism' became a buzzword, the people of Dominica had enticed visitors to their shores through the promotion of its untouched rainforests brimming with abundant wildlife and flora, the cascading waterfalls and crystal-clear rivers and rock pools, and the warmth and friendliness of its people. Even during the times of a robust banana industry, Dominicans made heritage preservation and promotion of local culture and cuisine a norm.

Dominicans are known to be some of the most hospitable people on earth and it is this very accolade which first and foremost drives its tourism industry. In 2007, Dominica was named the fourth happiest country in the world by *NEF's Happy Planet Index*. It has the highest number of centenarians per capita than anywhere else in the world and boasts a river for every day of the year … with an extra one for the tourists. People come here for Dominica and Dominicans. They do not seek the large resorts and casinos, or wish to spend every day soaking up the sun. Those who venture here are looking for a different type of Caribbean vacation, one which puts them in touch with nature.

Within its 305 square miles lie the National Forest Reserves, each offering a different charm. Morne Diablotin National Park (named after the island's highest peak) is home to Syndicate Forest and Syndicate Falls, the Sisserou parrot (National

FACING PAGE
The Emerald Pool is a tranquil location within Morne Trois Pitons National Park.

RIGHT
Hibiscus Valley Inn is nestled within lush surroundings.
Photos: Ian Brierley

Indian River boat
trip.

Ian Brierley / Hansib

Photo: Irvin C. Durand

Photo: Irvin C. Durand

bird) and the Jaco parrot; Cabrits National Park, with the historic Fort Shirley, offers an entire day of exploration and is extended by the Prince Rupert Bay Marine Reserve, a haven for divers and snorkellers; Morne Trois Pitons National Park is home to many sights and attractions including the Trois Pitons Trails, Emerald Pool, Middleham Falls, Boiling Lake and the Valley of Desolation. In 1997, this jewel in Dominica's crown was named by UNESCO as a World Heritage Site not only for its natural attributes but also for the work carried out by the National Parks and Forestry Division of the Ministry of Agriculture over the last four decades.

The Soufriere Scotts Head Marine Reserve, in the south-west of the island, completes the list of National Parks and is home to a number of the world's most dramatic dive sites. This submerged wonderland includes underwater hot springs that bubble up from the seabed and are affectionately referred to as 'champagne'.

The government's efforts in protecting the country's rich natural heritage has not gone unnoticed internationally, but mention must also be made of the numerous individuals and non-

Morne Trois Pitons National Park is home to many sights and attractions including the Valley of Desolation (above & left), where hikers can make the journey to the Boiling Lake, and the spectacular Middleham Falls (facing page).

Middleham Falls by Irvin C. Durand

The double
attraction of
Trafalgar Falls as
seen from the
viewing platform.
Ian Brierley / Hansib

government organisations such as the Dominica Conservation Association, the Society for Heritage Architectural Preservation & Enhancement, Dominica Watersports Association, Portsmouth Indian River Tour Guides Association and the Dominica Hotel & Tourism Association, to name but a few.

So, along with the sights and sounds of the natural world, the river bathing, kayaking, tubing, mountain biking and mountain hiking, rainforest trails and aerial trams, bird watching, scuba diving and sailing, Dominica can also boast the Caribbean's foremost whale-watching destination. The waters off the western coast record the region's highest species count of resident whales and dolphins.

Another major project currently under development is the Wai'tukubuli National Trail. Potentially Dominica's most significant eco-tourism attraction, it consists of a network of trails which traverse the island via the original tracks used by the early Kalinago settlers and the Neg Mawon (rebel slaves). The trail enables visitors to explore Dominica's interior for days at a time, stopping along the way at various communities and villages. It provides the perfect opportunity to gain first-hand knowledge of the way of life and culture of the Dominicans. This initiative ensures a genuine and unique experience for the visitor which, in turn, provides added employment and development opportunities for local people.

During the Carnival and Independence seasons, music infiltrates every corner of the towns and countryside. Food stalls, with their irresistible aromas, can be found on many curbs and street corners. Participants and visitors alike are bombarded with an intoxicating mix of sights, sounds, smells and flavours that delight the senses. It is a time when Dominica plays host to many artistic and literary events and musical performances including the World Creole Music Festival. Many Dominican bands and musicians have become

FACING PAGE
The peaceful courtyard at the Sutton Place Hotel belies the fact that it is in the heart of Roseau.

ABOVE RIGHT
Many stores throughout the capital have adapted to the increasing number of tourist arrivals.

RIGHT
The Zandoli Inn offers a natural and serene environment.
Photos: Ian Brierley

Wacky Rollers
Adventure Park
offers a fun-
packed tubing
experience down
the Layou River.
Ian Brierley / Hansib

The Islet Restaurant offers a fine menu of local and international cuisine.
Photo: Ian Brierley

A dive-master from Dive Dominica prepares his class for an unforgettable underwater experience.
Photo: Ian Brierley

FACING PAGE
Bathing in Ti Tou Gorge is one of Dominica's unique offerings.
Ian Brierley / Hansib

ABOVE RIGHT
Dominica is the Caribbean's leading whale-watching destination with the highest species count of resident whales and dolphins.

RIGHT
Fort Young Hotel.
Photo: Ian Brierley

famous throughout the Caribbean and on the international stage, and include such well-known acts as Nassio Fountaine, Exile One, Ophelia, Michel Henderson, Nellie St Harre, Grammacks and de Hunter. And at home, these renowned artistes share the stage with compatriots who ply their trade in traditional jing ping, la puet cabrit and calypso music to entertain Dominicans and tourists alike.

The celebration of the nation's 30th Anniversary of Independence (1978-2008) could provide an opportune moment for Dominica to focus more intensely on its spiritual and emotional growth. While using its resources to encourage more investment, it should also develop more opportunities in the areas of sport and wellness, as mandated in the government's 'Tourism Master Plan', and find ways to responsibly investigate and extract potential medical benefits which may lie dormant in the valleys, mountains and volcanic springs.

It has been a logical choice to protect and nurture an environment which has done the same for its inhabitants over the centuries. Dominicans around the world are demonstrating an iron-clad resolve to continue to work responsibly toward the development of this tiny island nation, which is so endowed with wonders rich and rare. ■

Investment opportunities in Dominica

RHODA LETANG

Investing in Dominica provides the opportunity to conduct business, while at the same allowing the investor to "defy the everyday" and enjoy the 'Nature Island of the Caribbean'.

The island's geology has contributed to the traditional predominance of agriculture as the main economic sector, with bananas as the primary crop. Agriculture has moved from being the main cash-generating sector of the economy during the early 1960s to the late 1980s, and is replaced by the tourism and services sectors. This can be attributed to an improvement in the level of education and private sector attempts to adjust to growing demands for services in a global economy.

The government has recognised this trend, and through a process of reform, is removing unnecessary inhibitors to private sector growth and investment, with the intent of establishing an enabling environment that will contribute to the success of all ventures in which Dominica has a competitive advantage.

The economy continues to show buoyancy, which is attributable to positive growth in the tourism, communications, construction and banking and insurance sectors. This trend is expected to continue in the medium term.

In addition to its programme for the diversification of the agricultural sector, the government continues to encourage expansion in manufacturing and agro-processing, and invites investments in tourism accommodation and resort facilities, particularly to take advantage of Dominica's ecological, natural and cultural tourism product. Similar opportunities exist in restaurant, duty-free shopping, tours, yachting facilities and recreational and entertainment operations such as visitor sites and attractions, theme parks, nightclubs and water sports.

Investments in the Information and Communications Technology (ICT) sector are prioritised as important and desired economic activities that can provide not only high quality jobs, but can take advantage of Dominica's advanced telecommunications systems, educated workforce and the many other benefits available to that sector.

As part of the economic diversification programme, Dominica has emerged as a premiere offshore financial centre in the Caribbean, offering investors a stable political and economic environment, accommodating legislation, an excellent telecommunications system and generous tax and customs duty exemptions.

Dominica's varied landscape and spectacular scenery present vast opportunities for real estate

FACING PAGE
Investment opportunities exist in duty-free shopping. The Archipelago Duty-Free Emporium in Roseau is a popular stop-off for cruise ship passengers.

RIGHT
National Bank of Dominica in Portsmouth.
Photos: Ian Brierley

Cruise ship passengers arriving in Roseau can take advantage of Dominica's ecological, natural and cultural delights with regular tours and excursions.

Ian Brierley / Hansib

development. Government has identified certain State and private lands as suitable for the development of high quality housing, hotels and resorts, tourism recreation, non-traditional agriculture and industrial and commercial parks. Opportunities exist for joint venture investments with private landowners throughout the island.

The island's natural attributes, which include verdant forests, dramatic sceneries, numerous rivers and waterfalls, along with a rich culture and heritage, proximity to the US mainland and an educated and skilled workforce, make it an ideal location for investments in film and media.

Improvements in air access and airport facilities will provide even greater opportunities for tourism visitation and investments. The upgrade of the airport is aimed at improving air access into Dominica by facilitating same-day connections from long haul destinations out of regional hubs such as Antigua, as night landing will be possible. A continued strong and aggressive tourism marketing programme is designed to support these initiatives.

INVESTMENT INCENTIVES

The government offers fiscal and other forms of concessions to encourage investments in development projects in the manufacturing, agri-business, tourism, ICT and services sectors. Generally, concessions are granted based on the level of investment, export earnings potential, employment and human resource development. Companies which qualify for fiscal incentives are allowed to import into Dominica all building materials, equipment, machinery, spare parts, raw and packaging materials used in production, free of all duties and taxes.

It is important to note, that foreign nationals are allowed to repatriate all of their earnings from Dominica. There is also no Estate Tax, Death Tax or Capital Gains Tax in Dominica, which is an attractive incentive for potential investors. In

FACING PAGE
Well known for its verdant forests and mountainous terrain, Dominica also has a number of typically Caribbean beaches.
Cecil Clarke

ABOVE
Landing at Melville Hall Airport. Improvements in air access and airport facilities will provide even greater opportunities for investments in tourism.
Irvin C. Durand

RIGHT
Arrivals at Melville Hall Airport.
Ian Brierley / Hansib

Dominica's varied landscape and spectacular scenery present opportunities for the development of high quality housing, hotels, eco-lodges such as Gachette's Rainforest Cottages and Guesthouse.

Ian Brierley / Hansib

ABOVE
The Emerald
Pool. Lush
rainforests and
numerous rivers,
pools and
waterfalls,
provide many
opportunities for
tour operators.
Irvin C. Durand

FACING PAGE
Fort Young Hotel.
Dominica invites
investments in
tourism
accommodation
and resort
facilities.
Ian Brierley / Hansib

addition, Dominica has a tax treaty with Great Britain, the United States and CARICOM countries to prevent double taxation of income earned in Dominica. Investors are also constitutionally protected from confiscation and arbitrary seizure of property.

The government recognises that in addition to investment incentives it must engender the economic, social and political environment that will permit medium to long-term viability of investments. Consequently, the government is delivering effective training to the populace, promoting Dominica as an ideal investment location, contributing to the positive evolution of the financial sector, fostering the development of reliable and affordable utilities, creating job opportunities and astutely managing the fiscal position.

INVEST DOMINICA AUTHORITY

The Invest Dominica Authority (IDA) is a newly-established Statutory Authority created by an Act of Parliament in 2007 for the promotion, facilitation and stimulation of foreign and local investment in Dominica. The IDA facilitates value-added business activity in Dominica from initial contact to operational reality. Assistance is available for research in providing data and investment information, identifying business opportunities and sources of financing, and arranging key contacts. During the planning stage, the IDA can help in all negotiations, from the screening process to the final evaluation and approval of investment proposals. The authority will co-ordinate the approval process and will act as a clearing-house for obtaining all necessary permits and licences from relevant government ministries, agencies and departments. The IDA makes representation to Government for the granting of fiscal incentives and other concessions and for approval of licences to operate value added businesses in Dominica. The relevant application forms are available on request.

The IDA is, basically, a one-stop source for doing business in Dominica. For more information, visit www.investdominica.dm

Bienvenue à la Dominique

MARCELLA LAROCQUE-MENAL

FRANCAIS / FRENCH

S'il vous arrive de trouver le vert un peu terne, c'est sans doute que vous n'avez jamais eu l'occasion d'être ébloui par la multitude de tons de vert qui font les couleurs de la Dominique. Surnommée "l'île Nature des Antilles" en raison de ses paysages demeurés intacts et de ses vastes forêts, la Dominique est la plus septentrionale des îles du Vent. "Je ne peux pas croire qu'en termes de splendeur et de majesté l'on puisse trouver quelque endroit au monde capable de rivaliser avec la chaîne de montagnes boisées de la Dominique," écrivait Alex Waugh en 1948. "C'est vert, tout vert."

La Dominique est l'île la plus montagneuse des Petites Antilles et abrite le sommet le plus élevée des Antilles orientales (Morne Diablotins). C'est aussi l'une des îles les plus "jeunes" des Antilles, puisqu'elle continue d'être formée par son activité géothermique et volcanique. On peut voir s'opérer ce processus au Boiling Lake, le second plus grand lac bouillonnant du monde.

En 1493, Christophe Colomb atteignit les côtes l'île et la baptisa du nom du jour de sa "découverte", Dominica (du latin dominicus – dimanche). Mais les habitants précolombiens de l'île – les Caribes – l'avaient déjà nommée Wai'tu kubuli, qui signifie "Son corps est grand". Ardemment défendue par les Caribes (ou Kalinagos), la Dominique fut l'une des dernières îles de la région à être colonisée par les Européens. Aujourd'hui, le pays est la patrie de l'unique population caribe survivante aux Antilles orientales. Ce sont les descendants des tous premiers habitants de la région, qui ont donné leur nom aux Caraïbes.

Dans une volonté de reconnaître l'importance de ces premiers habitants, la Dominique a pris l'importante décision de protéger les droits fonciers de sa population caribe. En 1903, on lui attribua une zone de 1500 hectares à laquelle on donna l'appellation de "réserve caribe". Connu aujourd'hui sous le nom de Territoire caribe, ce domaine protégé abrite huit petits villages où les Kalinagos entretiennent un lien étroit avec la nature à travers des coutumes et un savoir transmis de génération en génération. Ils y cultivent des techniques artisanales traditionnelles, telles que la fabrication de canoës ou la vannerie. Bien que coexistant tout à fait aisément en ces temps modernes, ils demeurent fidèles à l'esprit et à la culture de leurs ancêtres.

Les paysages verdoyants de la Dominique fournissent un parfait décor aux richesses de sa flore et de sa faune sauvages. Souvent décrite comme la plus variée des îles des Antilles orientales, la Dominique abrite certaines espèces qui n'existent nulle part ailleurs, tel le perroquet sisserou, l'oiseau national. Sous la surface, les fonds marins offrent un spectacle tout aussi grisant. L'île a été classée parmi les cinq plus beaux sites de plongée dans le monde, et sa faune marine est considérée par beaucoup comme la plus riche du monde. Ses eaux sont par ailleurs visitées par non moins de sept espèces de baleines, faisant de la Dominique le premier site d'observation de baleines des Antilles.

L'île Nature des Antilles est un lieu tout à fait intact. On dit parfois que si Christophe Colomb revenait visiter les Antilles aujourd'hui, la seule île qu'il reconnaîtrait serait la Dominique. Ceci ne veut aucunement dire qu'elle soit sous-développée, mais qu'elle a su au contraire garder intacts ses paysages et sa beauté naturelle.

La Dominique est une destination authentique, sans ingrédients artificiels, tout simplement naturelle. Le Boiling Lake en est un exemple typique : on ne peut contempler ce cratère bouillonnant qu'après avoir marché plus de trois heures depuis le village le plus proche. Onze montagnes offrent aux randonneurs des itinéraires de difficultés diverses ; les 365 rivières de l'île traversent son relief accidenté dans tous les sens pour alimenter des chutes d'eau spectaculaires que l'on atteint par des chemins de randonnée dont le degré de difficulté varie de relativement facile à difficile.

Les visiteurs disposent par ailleurs d'un vaste éventail de solutions d'hébergement : on trouvera dans l'île des hôtels contemporains, des pensions de famille et des sites de vacances, mais aussi des auberges et des refuges éloignés de tout où les invités seront réveillés chaque matin par une symphonie tropicale donnée par des oiseaux aux couleurs éclatantes, dans une végétation luxuriante pleine de fleurs exotiques. En bref, la Dominique est un lieu privilégié pour les écotouristes.

La Dominique accueille chaque année le Festival mondial de musique créole, qui célèbre "trois nuits de rythmes endiablés" sur une musique cadence, zouk, bouyon, kompas, zydeco, reggae, soukous et soca interprétée par des musiciens locaux, régionaux et internationaux. Le "Real Mas" est un carnaval qui se tient juste avant la saison du carême et lors duquel sont organisés des concours de calypso et de costumes, ponctués par deux journées de fête dans les rues. Ont lieu également de nombreux festivals de villages, parmi lesquels le Dive Fest, le festival Emancipation, le Festival des arts de la Dominique, le Pork Fest, le Rabbit Fest, le Goat Fest, le Fish Fest et le Titiwe Fest, qui célèbrent des coutumes, traditions et nourritures locales demeurant bien présentes à la Dominique.

La culture dominicaine est une trame somptueuse et vivante, profondément intégrée à la vie quotidienne de ses habitants. Des habitants qui vous réservent un accueil cordial et chaleureux : il est normal de rencontrer un Dominicain pour la première fois et d'être salué par un large sourire.

Venez à la Dominique y apprécier sa nature, goûter à l'accueil et à l'hospitalité de ses habitants, et découvrir par vous-même l'un des secrets les mieux gardés des Antilles.

Willkommen auf Dominica

MARCELLA LAROCQUE-MENAL

DEUTSCH / GERMAN

Wenn Sie jemals dachten, die Farbe grün wäre eintönig, dann haben Sie sicher noch nie die Tausenden Grünschattierungen gesehen, wie sie auf Dominica zu finden sind. Wegen seiner üppigen Wälder und unberührten Gebiete auch unter dem Namen „Naturinsel der Karibik" bekannt, ist Dominica die nördlichste der Windward Islands. „Ich glaube nicht, dass es irgendwo auf Erden einen Ort gibt, der es mit der Pracht und Schönheit der waldbedeckten Berge auf Dominica aufnehmen kann," schrieb Alex Waugh in 1948. „Sie sind grün, überall grün."

Dominica hat von den Inseln der Kleinen Antillen die meisten Berge, und auch der höchste Berg der östlichen Karibik (Morne Diablotins) befindet sich hier. Sie ist außerdem eine der ‚jüngsten' Karibikinseln, die sie sich aufgrund vulkanischer Aktivitäten noch immer weiterbildet. Dieser Prozess ist auch am Boiling Lake zu beobachten, dem zweitgrößten thermisch aktiven See der Welt.

1493 besuchte Christopher Kolumbus die Insel und benannte sie nach dem Tag seiner ‚Entdeckung', Dominica (Lateinisch für ‚Sonntag'). Allerdings hatten die Ureinwohner, die vor Kolumbus' Ankunft auf der Insel lebten – die Kariben – diese schon Wai'tukubuli genannt, was so viel bedeutet wie ‚hoch ist ihre Gestalt'. Da sich die Kariben (oder Kalinago) erbittert wehrten, war Dominica eine der letzten Inseln der Region, die von den Europäern kolonialisiert wurde. Heute leben auf der Insel die letzten noch verbliebenen Kariben der östlichen Karibik. Sie sind die Nachkommen der ersten Ureinwohner der Region, die der Karibik ihren Namen gaben.

Um die Bedeutung dieser ersten Siedler zu unterstreichen, unternahm Dominica den wichtigen Schritt, die Besitzrechte der Kariben zu schützen. 1903 wurde auf einer Fläche von 1.500 ha das so genannte ‚Kariben-Reservat' eingerichtet. Dieses heute als ‚Carib Territory' bekannte, geschützte Gebiet besteht aus acht kleinen Dörfern, in denen die Kalinago ihre Liebe zur Natur durch jahrhundertealtes Wissen und überlieferte Bräuche pflegen. Hier verfeinern sie traditionelle Fähigkeiten wie den Kanubau oder das Korbflechten. Und auch wenn sie heute in der modernen Welt leben, bewahren sie weiterhin den Geist und die Kultur ihrer Vorfahren.

Dominicas grüne Landschaft bildet den perfekten Hintergrund für seine üppige Flora und Fauna. Sie wird oft als die mannigfaltigste der östlichen Karibikinseln beschrieben und einige Arten - wie die Kaiseramazone, der Nationalvogel der Insel – sind nur auf Dominica zu finden. Und auch unter der Oberfläche ist die Insel atemberaubend und birgt aufregende Abenteuer. Sie gilt weltweit als eines der fünf besten Tauchgebiete, und ihre Meeresflora und –fauna sogar als die beste der Welt. In den Gewässern um die Insel leben sieben Walarten, weshalb Dominica unter den Karibikinseln der führende Walbeobachtungsort ist.

Die Naturinsel der Karibik ist ein wahrlich

unberührter Ort. Man sagt, würde Kolumbus die Karibik heute wieder besuchen, er würde nur Dominica wiedererkennen. Das bedeutet nicht, dass die Insel unterentwickelt ist, sondern nur, dass sie ihre natürliche Schönheit und unberührte Landschaft bewahrt hat.

Dominica ist Natur pur, ohne künstliche Zusatzstoffe. Der Boiling Lake ist hierfür das beste Beispiel: hier zu stehen und in seinen kochenden Krater zu schauen, bedeutet, dass man mindestens drei Stunden Fußmarsch vom Rest der Zivilisation entfernt ist. Elf Berge bieten Wanderern verschiedene Herausforderungsgrade: 365 Flüsse durchkreuzen das raue Gelände der Insel und münden in mehreren spektakulären Wasserfällen, zu denen die Wanderungen von leicht bis mühselig variieren.

Besucher auf Dominica können aus vielen verschiedenen Unterkünften wählen: von modernen Hotels, Gasthäusern und Resorts bis hin zu atemberaubenden Wildnis-Herbergen und –Refugien, in denen die Gäste jeden Morgen inmitten üppiger Vegetation und exotischer Blumen von einer tropischen Symphonie, aufgeführt von farbenprächtigen Vögeln, geweckt werden. Kurz gesagt, ist Dominica ein Zufluchtsort für Ökotouristen.

Dominica veranstaltet jährlich das World Creole Music Festival und zelebriert „drei Nächte pulsierender Rhythmen" zu den Klängen der Cadence, Zouk, Bouyon, Kompas, Zydeco, Reggae Soukous und Soca-Musik, die von lokalen, regionalen und internationalen Musikern gespielt wird. ‚The Real Mas' heißt der kurz vor der Fastenzeit stattfindende Karneval, an dem Calypso- und Kostümwettbewerbe durchgeführt werden, und der mit einem zweitägigen Straßenfest endet. Zudem finden viele verschiedene Dorffeste statt, wie das Tauchfest, das Emancipation Festival, das Dominica Festival der Künste, das Schweine-Fest, Kaninchen-Fest, Ziegen-Fest, Fisch-Fest und Titiwe Fest, bei dem Dominicas Bräuche, Traditionen und Gerichte zelebriert werden.

Die dominicanische Kultur ist reichhaltig und dynamisch, und tief im täglichen Leben seiner Bewohner verankert. Und diese Bewohner sind einladend und freundlich; wann immer Sie einen Dominicaner zum ersten Mal treffen, werden Sie mit einem freundlichen Lächeln begrüßt.

Besuchen Sie Dominica, erleben Sie seine Natur, Freundschaft und Gastfreundlichkeit und überzeugen Sie sich selbst von diesem bestgehüteten Geheimnis der Karibik.

Benvenuto a Dominica

MARCELLA LAROCQUE-MENAL

ITALIANO / ITALIAN

Se pensi che il colore verde sia sopravvalutato, forse non hai mai avuto l'opportunità di ammirare le migliaia di sfumature verdi dell'isola Dominica. Conosciuta con il nome di 'Nature Island' dei Caraibi, per il suo territorio ricco di foreste e incontaminato, Dominica è la più settentrionale delle Windward Islands. "Non credo che esista al mondo un luogo di simile grandezza e solennità, caratterizzato da una successione di montagne ricoperte di foreste come quelle di Dominica", scrisse nel 1948 Alex Waugh, "È verde, tutto verde…".

Dominica è la più montuosa delle Lesser Antilles e ospita la montagna più alta dei Caraibi orientali (Morne Diablotins). È anche una delle isole dei Caraibi 'più giovani', in quanto viene tuttora formata dall'attività geotermica-vulcanica. Questo processo è molto evidente nel Boiling Lake, il secondo lago più grande del mondo attivo termicamente.

Cristoforo Colombo visitò l'isola nel 1493 e la battezzò con il nome del giorno in cui la scoprì, 'Dominica' (dal latino per domenica). Gli abitanti pre-colombiani dell'isola – i Carib – avevano comunque già assegnato un nome al territorio: Wai'tukubuli, che significa 'dal corpo alto'. Dominica fu tenacemente difesa dai Carib (chiamati anche Kalinago) e fu una delle ultime isole della regione ad essere colonizzate dagli Europei. Attualmente, il paese ospita le sole popolazioni Carib ancora presenti nei Caraibi orientali. Questi individui discendono dai primi abitanti della zona e il nome 'Caraibi' deriva da loro.

Per riconoscere l'importanza di questi primi coloni, Dominica fece l'importante passo di proteggere i diritti di proprietà terriera delle popolazioni Carib. Una superficie di quasi 15 km² fu designata, nel 1903, come 'Riserva Carib'. Questa regione protetta, chiamata oggi 'Territorio Carib' consiste di otto piccoli villaggi in cui le popolazioni Kalinago mantengono la propria affinità con la natura, grazie a conoscenze e costumi trasmessi da generazione a generazione. I Carib possono quindi continuare a dedicare tutta la propria attenzione ad attività tradizionali, come la produzione di canoe e l'intreccio di panieri. Questi popoli coesistono tranquillamente nei tempi moderni, ma mantengono ancora vivo il proprio impegno nei confronti dello spirito e cultura degli antenati.

Il verdeggiante paesaggio di Dominica è il luogo ideale per le molte specie di flora e fauna selvagge. Alcune specie vivono soltanto in questa zona, spesso descritta come la più diversificata isola dei Caraibi orientali, come il pappagallo Sisserou, l'uccello nazionale di Dominica. L'isola è altrettanto spettacolare sotto la superficie, dove i visitatori possono vivere esperienze davvero allettanti. Dominica è stata classificata come una delle cinque destinazioni più importanti del mondo e la vita marina dell'isola viene solitamente considerata la migliore al mondo. Le acque che circondano l'isola sono anche visitate da sette specie di balene: Domenica è la principale destinazione dei Caraibi per avvistare le balene.

La 'Nature Island' è certamente un luogo incontaminato. Si racconta che se Cristoforo Colombo visitasse oggi i Caraibi, riconoscerebbe soltanto l'isola di Dominica. Questo non significa certamente che l'isola sia sottosviluppata, ma piuttosto che Dominica mantiene la sua bellezza naturale e paesaggio incontaminato.

Dominica offre un'esperienza autentica e naturale, senza ingredienti artificiali. Il primo esempio è il Boiling Lake: quando ti soffermi a guardare questo cratere gorgogliante, sei almeno a tre ore di distanza a piedi dal resto della civilizzazione. Hiking di varie difficoltà è disponibile su undici montagne; i 365 fiumi dell'isola attraversano il terreno accidentato e si immergono in varie spettacolari cascate raggiungibili attraverso percorsi di difficoltà da relativa a estrema.

Diversi tipi di alloggio sono disponibili per i visitatori di Dominica: alberghi contemporanei, bed and breakfast, resort, spettacolari pensioni nella natura incontaminata e rifugi in cui gli ospiti vengono destati ogni mattina da una sinfonia tropicale, suonata da uccelli coloratissimi, nel bel mezzo di una vegetazione lussuriosa e di fiori esotici. L'isola è quindi una destinazione per i turisti ecologici.

Dominica è la sede annuale del Festival mondiale della musica creola, che celebra le 'tre notti di ritmi pulsanti', al suono di musica a cadenza, zouk, bouyon, kompas, zydeco, reggae soukous e soca eseguita da musicisti locali, regionali e internazionali. **'The Real Mas'**, il festival del Carnevale che ha luogo prima del periodo quaresimale, organizza gare di calipso e allestimenti, e culmina in due giorni di baldoria per le strade. Hanno luogo anche molti festival annuali nei singoli villaggi, come 'Dive Fest', 'Emancipation Festival', 'Dominica Festival of Arts', 'Pork Fest', 'Rabbit Fest', 'Goat Fest', 'Fish Fest' e 'Titiwe Fest'; tutti questi eventi celebrano i costumi, le tradizioni e i cibi locali che prosperano a Dominica.

La cultura dominicana è un affresco ricco e vibrante, profondamente integrato nella vita quotidiana dei suoi abitanti. E le popolazioni locali sono cortesi e ospitali; potrai sempre incontrare un dominicano per la prima volta ed essere accolto con un sorriso caloroso.

Vieni quindi a Dominica e vivi la natura, l'amicizia e l'ospitalità, e scopri in prima persona uno dei segreti più nascosti dei Caraibi.

Bienvenido a Dominica

MARCELLA LAROCQUE-MENAL

ESPAÑOL / SPANISH

Si alguna vez pensó que lo verde es decepcionante, es muy probable que nunca se haya sentido sobrecogido por las miles de tonalidades de verde que existen en Dominica. Conocida como la "Isla de la Naturaleza del Caribe" por su terreno casi virgen y cubierto de bosque, Dominica es la más septentrional de las Islas de Barlovento. "Me resulta difícil creer que haya algo en el mundo que pueda rivalizar en grandiosidad y majestuosidad con la cantidad de montañas cubiertas de bosque que hay en Dominica", escribió Alex Waugh en 1948. "Es verde, totalmente verde".

Dominica es la isla más montañosa de las Antillas Menores y la que alberga la montaña más alta del Caribe Oriental (Morne Diablotins). También se la conoce como la isla más "joven" del Caribe, ya que aún se está formando mediante actividad geotérmica volcánica. Este proceso se puede ver en el Boiling Lake, el segundo lago más grande del mundo con actividad térmica.

En 1493, Cristóbal Colón visitó la isla y le dio el nombre del día de su "descubrimiento": Dominica (derivado de la palabra latina que designa al domingo). Sin embargo, sus habitantes precolombinos (los caribes) ya tenían un nombre para la isla: Wai'tukubuli, que significa "alto es su cuerpo". Los caribes (o kalinagos) la defendieron con fiereza y Dominica fue una de las últimas islas de la región en ser colonizada por los europeos. Hoy en día, el país acoge a la única población de caribes que queda en el Caribe Oriental. Son los descendentes de los primeros pobladores humanos de la región, los cuales dieron nombre al Caribe.

Para reconocer la relevancia de estos primeros pobladores, Dominica tomó la importante decisión de proteger los derechos a las tierras del pueblo caribe. En 1903, se designó como "Reserva caribe" un área de 1.500 hectáreas. Hoy se la conoce como el territorio caribe y es una región protegida que consta de ocho comunidades pequeñas donde los kalinagos mantienen su afinidad con la naturaleza mediante el conocimiento y las costumbres heredados a través de generaciones. En ella continúan desarrollando sus habilidades tradicionales, como la fabricación de canoas y la cestería. Aunque coexisten fácilmente en los tiempos modernos, los kalinagos todavía permanecen fieles al espíritu y la cultura de sus antecesores.

El paisaje verde de Dominica proporciona el marco perfecto para una flora y una fauna exuberantes. A menudo se la describe como la isla más diversa del Caribe Oriental y algunas especies sólo existen en Dominica, como el loro Sisserou, que es el ave nacional. Bajo la superficie, donde emocionantes aventuras atraen al visitante, la isla es igual de extraordinaria. Se la ha clasificado como uno de los cinco principales destinos mundiales de buceo, y su vida marina se suele considerar como la mejor del mundo. Las aguas que rodean la isla también reciben la visita de siete especies de ballenas, lo cual convierte a Dominica en el principal destino en el Caribe para la observación de ballenas.

La Isla de la Naturaleza del Caribe es un destino que indudablemente conserva su belleza natural. Se ha dicho que si Cristóbal Colón visitase el Caribe actual, la única isla que reconocería sería Dominica. Esto no quiere decir para nada que la isla esté subdesarrollada, sino que ha mantenido su belleza natural y su paisaje impecable.

Dominica es auténtica, sin ingredientes artificiales y sencillamente natural. El Boiling Lake es un excelente ejemplo: si se asoma a este cráter hirviendo, estará al menos a tres horas a pie del resto de la civilización. Once montañas proporcionan diversos grados de desafío a los excursionistas, mientras que los 365 ríos de la isla entrecruzan el terreno escabroso y nutren varias cataratas espectaculares. Las excursiones a las mismas van desde las relativamente fáciles a las arduas.

Dominica también cuenta con una gran oferta de alojamiento: desde hoteles modernos, pensiones y centros turísticos a posadas extraordinarias en zonas salvajes y retiros donde los huéspedes se despiertan cada mañana con una sinfonía tropical a cargo de pájaros de brillante plumaje, en medio de una tupida vegetación y de flores exóticas. Resumiendo, Dominica es un paraíso para el ecoturismo.

Dominica es la sede del Festival Mundial de Música Criolla que celebra "tres noches de compases palpitantes" a ritmos de cadencia, zouk, bouyon, kompa, zydeco, reggae soukous y soca que aportan músicos locales, regionales e internacionales. El "Real Mas", el carnaval que tiene lugar antes de la Cuaresma, da cabida a competiciones de calipso y esplendor y culmina con dos días de jolgorio callejero. También hay numerosos festivales de localidades individuales, como Dive Fest, el Festival de la Independencia, Dominica Festival of Arts, Pork Fest, Rabbit Fest, Fish Fest y Titiwe Fest, los cuales celebran las costumbres, tradiciones y gastronomía locales que prosperan en Dominica.

La cultura dominicana es un rico y efervescente tapiz que se encuentra profundamente enraizado en las vidas cotidianas de sus gentes. Y la gente en cuestión es acogedora y amistosa: siempre se puede esperar un saludo con una cálida sonrisa al encontrarse con un dominicano por primera vez.

Así que venga a Dominica a vivir la naturaleza, la amistad y la hospitalidad y a conocer por sí mismo uno de los secretos mejor guardados del Caribe.

Businesses in the capital are given a boost with the arrival of a cruise ship.
Photo: Ian Brierley / Hansib

GOVERNMENT DIRECTORY

Prime Minister & Minister for Finance, Social Security & Foreign Affairs
Hon. Roosevelt Skerrit

Trade, Industry, Consumer Affairs, Private Sector Relations, CARICOM, OECS & Diaspora Affairs
Senator Hon. Dr. John Collin McIntyre

Tourism, Legal Affairs & Civil Aviation
Hon. Ian Douglas

Agriculture, Fisheries & Forestry
Hon. Matthew J. Walter

Education, Human Resource Development, Sports & Youth Affairs
Hon. Vince Henderson

Health & the Environment
Hon. John Fabien

Housing, Lands & Telecommunications
Hon. Reginald Austrie

Public Works & Infrastructural Development
Hon. Ambrose George

Public Utilities, Energy, Ports & the Public Service
Senator Hon. Charles Savarin

Carib Affairs
Hon. Kelly Graneau

Economic Development & Urban Renewal
Hon. Julius Timothy

Community Development, Culture, Gender Affairs & Information
Hon. Loreen Bannis-Roberts

National Security, Immigration, Labour
Hon. Rayburn Blackmoore

Attorney General
Hon. Francine Baron-Royer

Parliamentary Secretary - Public Works & Infrastructural Development
Hon. Urban Baron

Parliamentary Secretary – Office of the Prime Minister (To assist with Foreign Affairs)
Hon. Petter Saint Jean

Parliamentary Secretary – Education, Human Resource Development, Sports & Youth Affairs (To assist with Youth & Sports)
Hon. Ian Pinard

CONSULAR OFFICES

GUADELOUPE

Mr Felix Cherdieu D'Alexis, Honorary Consul
21 Rue Gambetta, 97110 Pointe-a-Pitre
Tel/Fax: 011 590 590 82 01 57

INDIA

Mr Ramakant Shukla, Honorary Consul
283 Gulmohar Enclave
New Delhi – 110-049
Tel: 011 91 11 688 25 95
Fax: 011 91 11 26 86 25 95

JAMAICA

Mr Emile George, Honorary Consul
21 East Street
Kingston
Tel: 876 702 1830 / 876 922 2283

MARTINIQUE

Mr Mark Frampton
Rue Aigue Marine
Bat A2 rue de la Dorsale
97200 Fort de France
Tel: 011 86 10 65 32 65 20

SWEDEN

Mr Raoul Smitt, Honorary Consul
Advokatijirman Smitt A.B., Hamngatan 11
S-11147 Stockholm
Tel: 468 678 0770. Fax: 468 678 0780
Email: lawoffices@smitt.se

UNITED STATES OF AMERICA

Consulate of the Commonwealth of Dominica
Suite H, 800 Second Avenue
New York, N.Y 10017
Tel: 212 949 0853/4, 212 599 8478
Fax: 212 661 0979
Email: dmaun@undp.org
Mrs Barbara Dailey, Consul General

EMBASSIES

BELGIUM

Embassies of the Eastern Caribbean States and Missions to the European Communities
42 Rue de Livourne
1050 Brussels
Tel: 011 02 534 2611, 011 322 534 2611
Fax: 011 322 539 4009
Email: ecs.embassies@skynet.be
His Excellency George Bullen, Ambassador Extraordinary and Plenipotentiary

CUBA

Embassy of the Commonwealth of Dominica
Havana
His Excellency Clarkson Thomas, Ambassador Extraordinary and Plenipotentiary

PEOPLES REPUBLIC OF CHINA

Embassy of the Commonwealth of Dominica
LA o6 Liangmaqiao
Diplomatic Residence Compound
No. 22 Dongfangdong Road
Chaoyang District
Beijing
Tel: 010 653 208 38
Fax: 010 653 208 48
Email: dominica@dominicaembassy.com
His Excellency David Hsiu, Ambassador Extraordinary and Plenipotentiary

UNITED STATES OF AMERICA

Embassy of the Commonwealth of Dominica
3216 New Mexico N.W.
Washington D.C. 20016
Tel: 1 202 364 6781 / 202 364 6790
Fax: 202 364 6791
Email: embdomdc@aol.com
Judith Ann Role, Charge d'Affaires

HIGH COMMISSIONS

CANADA

High Commission for the Countries of the Organisation of Eastern Caribbean States
130 Albert Street
Suite 700
Ottawa
Ontario K1P 5G4
Tel: 1 613 236 8952
Fax: 1 613 236 6042
Email: echcc@travel_net.com
His Excellency Brendon Browne, High Commissioner

UNITED KINGDOM

Dominica High Commission
1 Collingham Gardens
London SW5 OHW
Tel: 011 44 207 370 5194
Fax: 011 44 207 372 8743
Email: dominicahighcom@btconnect.com
Agnes Adonis, Acting High Commissioner

REPRESENTATION

DOMINICA

Discover Dominica Authority
Valley Road
Roseau
Phone: (767) 448-2045
Call toll free: 1 866 522 4057
Fax: (767) 448-5840
Email: tourism@dominica.dm

GERMANY, AUSTRIA & SWITZERLAND

Fremdenverkehrsburo von Dominica
Postfach 140223
D-70072 Stuttgart, Germany
Phone: + 49 711 26346624
Fax: + 49 711 5053534
Email: Dominica@tropical-consult.de

UNITED KINGDOM

The Saltmarsh Partnership
The Copperfields
25D Copperfield Street
London, SE1 0EN
Phone: 020 7928 1600
Fax: 020 7928 1700
Freephone: 0800 012 1467
Email: dominica@saltmarshpr.co.uk

UNITED STATES & CANADA

Imagery Creative Communications
6915 Red Road, Suite 226
Coral Gardens, FL 33143
Tel: 305 667 4468
Fax: 305 667 2635
Email: josh@imagerycreative.com

OVERSEAS ASSOCIATIONS

CANADA

Commonwealth of Dominica Ontario
Association
648-A Yonge Street, Suite #6
Toronto
Ontario M4Y 2A6
Tel: 905 433 0916
Fax: 905 433 1696

UNITED KINGDOM

Dominica UK Association (DUKA)
NACR Centre
627-633 Barking Road
Plaistow
London E13 9EZ
Tel: +44 (0) 20 8925 2025
Fax: +44 (0) 20 8925 2025

Dominica Oversea Nationals Association
(DONA)
11 Nemoure Road Acton
London W3
Tel: +44 (0) 20 8992 0142
Email: donaassoc@hotmail.com

UNITED STATES OF AMERICA

Tampa Bay Dominica Organization
4006 East Regnas Avenue
Tampa, Florida 33617
Tel: (813) 988-0885

Dominica Multi-Purpose Organization Inc.
10613 NW 10th Street
Pembroke Pines
Florida 33026
Tel: 954 588 8095

Dominicans of South Florida
777 N.W. 155 Lane, Apt. 603
Miami, Florida 33169

Dominica Association of Midwestern USA
(DAMUSA)
P.O. Box 378356
Jackson Park Station
Chicago IL, 60637-9998

Baystate Dominica Association
P.O. Box 260288
Mattapan, MA 02126
Tel: 617-296-9626

Sisserou Social Club - Boston
27 Webster Street
Randolph, MA 02368
Tel:(781)-961-1071

The Caribbean Foundation of Boston Inc.
317 Blue Hill Avenue
Dorchester MA 02121

Dominica Emerald Organization of New
Jersey
38 Hartgrove Terrace
Irvington
New Jersey, 07111

Dominica Sisserou International Group
P.O. Box 611, Maplecrest Station
Maplewood, NJ 07040

Dominica Patriots
119-46 223rd Street, Cambria Height
LI., New York 11411
Tel: (718) 978-8965

Dominica American Relief & Development
Association Inc. (DARDA)
2317 Hoffman Avenue
Elmont, New York, 11003

Five Seasons Social Club
90-02 Vanderveer Street
Queens Village, NY 11428
Tel: (718) 776-2579

Commonwealth of Dominica Improvement
Association (CODIA)
4351 Matilda Avenue
Bronx
New York, 10469
Tel: (718) 654-6690 or 718-654-9891

Moka
120-19 234th Street
Cambria Heights, New York, 11411
Tel: (516) 745-8127

The Caribbean Relief and Scholarship
Fund
86 Thayer Street, Suite 1J
New York, New York, 10040
Tel: (212) 942-8198
Fax: (212) 294-4700

Colihaut in Focus
3330 Colden Avenue
Bronx, New York 10467

Dominica New York Organization
1530 Sheridon Avenue, Apt. 6G
Bronx, New York 10457
Tel: (718) 731-1613

Dominica Academy of Arts and Sciences
(DAAS)
1522 Braden Avenue
Wilmington DE 19808
Email: President@daacadmy.org
Web: http:www.da_academy.org

Sensay.com
90-03 179 Street
Jamaica, New York 11432

Escape Lounge
1687 Watson Avenue
Bronx, NY 10472

Exodus
461 Riverdale Avenue, #7H
Yonkers, NY 10705

Dominica Association of Seventh Day
Adventists in the United States
P.O. Box 289
East Norwich, NY 11749
Tel: 646-289-9943
Fax: 646-289-9942

Dominica Houston Association
8449 W. Bellfort, Suite 136
Houston, TX 77071

INTERNATIONAL DIALLING CODE: 767

EMERGENCY NUMBERS

FIRE / POLICE / AMBULANCE: 999

POLICE FORCE: 448-2222

FIRE & AMBULANCE SERVICE: 448-2889

CRISIS HOTLINE: 1-800-4357

Princess Margaret Hospital: 448-2231

APARTMENTS / COTTAGES

Caprice Studio Apt and Cottages
Canefield/Elmshall
Tel: 448-0549
Fax: 449-0009
Website: www.capriceapartments.com

Caribbean Sea View Apartments
Mero
Tel: 449-7572
Email: info@caribbeanseaview.com
Website: www.carribbeanseaview.com

Casaropa Apartment
Portsmouth
Tel: 445-5277
Email: casaropa@marpin.dm
Website: www.casaropa.com

Chez Ophelia
Copt Hall
Tel: 448-3438
Fax: 448-3433
Email: chezophelia@cwdom.dm
Website: www.chezophelia.com/

Cocoa Cottage
Shawford
Tel: 448-0412
Email: cocoacottages@cwdom.dm
Website: www.cocoacottages.com

Crescent Moon Cabins
River La Croix
Tel: 449-3449
Email: jeanviv@cwdom.dm
Website: www.crescentmooncabins.com

D'Auchamps Cottages
Trafalgar
Tel: 448-3346
Email: honychurchs@cwdom.dm
Website: www.avirtualdominica.com

Dominica's Sea View Apartments
Calibishie
Tel: 317-1843. Fax: 445-8074
E: info@dominicasseaviewapartments.com
Website: www.dominicasguesthouse.com

Eileen Shillingford Apartment
St Aroment
Tel: 448-2986
Email: yannick@cwdom.dm

Emerald View Apts
Canefield
Tel: 449-3462. Fax: 276-1404
Email: colombo104@hotmail.com

Evertons View
Loubiere
Tel: 448-2788
Email: jollyt@cwdom.dm
Email: service@jollysonline.com

Exotica
Gommier
Tel: 448-8839. Fax: 448-8829
Email: exotica@cwdom.dm
Website: www.exotica-cottages.com

Gachette Cottages
Pond Casse
Tel: 446-0700
Email: info@gachettedominica.com
Website: www.gachettecottages.com

Ginger Lily Cottage
Riviere Cyrique
Tel: 446-1170
Email: gingerinfo@hotmail.com
Website: www.ginger-lily.com

Gallette Seaside Cottages
Soufriere
Tel: 449-8181
Email: natureidive@cwdom.dm
Website: www.natureislanddive.com

Grace Apartment
Wotten Waven
Tel: 448-2934. Fax: 448-8977
Email: elgee@cwdom.dm
Website: www.avirtualdominica.com/
graceapartments

Hampstead House
Hampstead
Tel: 445-5639
Email: mendoug@cwdom.dm

Harmony Villa
Pond Casse
Tel: 276-3804
Email: carlaarmour@hotmail.com
Website: www.harmonyvilla.com

Hodgesview Cottages
Portsmouth
Tel: 445-7061
Email: information@hodgesview.com
Website: www.hodgesview.com

Itassi Cottages
Morne Bruce
Tel: 449-8700
Email: sutton2@cwdom.dm
Website: www.avirtualdominica.com/itassi

Lamani Resort
Portsmouth
Email: lamaniresort@cwdom.dm
Website: www.lamaniresort.com

Ocean View Apartments
Scotts Head
Tel: 449-8266. Fax: 449-8266
Email: oceanview_apts@hotmail.com
Website: www.avirtualdominica.com/
oceanview_apt

Point Baptiste Cottage
Calibishie
Tel: 445-7379
Email: manager@pointebaptiste.com
Website: www.pointebaptiste.com

Rainbow Village Cottages
Cochrane
Tel: 449-2903
Email: rainbowvillagedm@yahoo.com
Website: www.avirtualdominica.com/
rainbowvillage

Rainforest Paradise
Belles
Tel: 449-3074
Email: rainforestparadise@cwdom.dm
Website: www.rainforestparadise.com

Rainforest Retreat
6 Shawford Estate
Tel: 449-9540
Fax: 448-7059
Email: rachel@ourdominica.com
Website: www.ourdominica.com

Rainforest ShangriLa Resort
Wotten Waven
Tel: 440-5093
Fax: 616-9322
Email: Shangrila@cwdom.dm
Website:
www.rainforestshangrilaresort.com

Sea Cliff Cottages
Calibishie
Tel: 445-7008. Fax: 445-7322
Email: seacliff@cwdom.dm
Website: www.dominica-cottages.com

Stowe Seaside Resort
Stowe Estate
Tel: 446-3647
Email: fadellec@cwdom.dm

Surf Song Cottages (Fred Oesch's Property)
Delices
Email: surfsongcottages@gmail.com
Website: www.surfsongcottages.com

Tia's Bamboo Cottages
Wotten Waven
Tel: 448-1998
Fax: 225-8591
Email: tiacottages@hotmail.com
Website: www.tiabamboocottages.com

Verandas View
Calibishie
Tel: 445-8900
Email: reserve@lodgingdominica.com
Website: www.lodgingdominica.com

White Cottages
Glasgow
Tel: 448-2028

ARCHITECTS

Agar & Johnson
Lahaut Loubiere, P.O. Box 61, Roseau
Tel: (767) 448 2282. Fax: (767) 448 2282

Andre Lennard
12 Franklyn Lane, Goodwill, Roseau
Tel: (767) 449 8099
Fax: (767) 440 2499

Architect ERA
P.O. Box 0872, 30 Federation Drive
Goodwill
Tel: (767) 245 0930
Fax: (767) 500 8600
Email: royere@marpin.

Architectropics
9 Hillsborough & Old Street, Roseau
Tel: (767) 448 2336
Fax: (767) 448 5911

Baptiste & Associates Ltd
64 Kennedy Avenue, P.O. Box 500, Roseau
Tel: (767) 448 1999
Fax: (767) 448 1930
Email: bapassoc@cwdom.dm

McKenzie Architectural & Construction
Services Inc.
12 Virgin Lane, P.O. Box 514, Roseau
Tel: (767) 448 1941. Fax: (767) 448 1941
Email: Mckenzies@cwdom.dm
Website: www.macservicesinc.com

BANKS

Bank of Nova Scotia
28 Hillsborough Street, Box 520, Roseau
Tel: 767 448 5800. Fax: 767 448 5805
Email: bns.dominica@scotiabank.com
Website: www.scotiabank.com

First Caribbean International Bank
Old Street, P.O. Box 4, Roseau
Tel: 767 448 2571
Fax: 757 448 3471
Website: www.firstcaribbeanbank.com

National Bank of Dominica Ltd
Hillsborough Street, P.O. Box 271, Roseau
Tel: 767- 448 4401
Fax: 767- 448 3982
Email: ncbdom@cwdom.dm
Website: www.nbdominica.dm

Royal Bank of Canada
Bay Front, P.O. Box 19, Roseau
Tel: 767 448 2771
Fax: 767 448 5398
Email: rbcdominica@cwdom.dm
Website: www.royalbank.com

CAMPING GROUNDS

Rosalie Forest Eco Lodge
Rosalie
Tel: 446-1886
Email: info@rosalieforest.com
Website: www.rosalieforest.com

ENGINEERS

Ace Engineering Ltd
18 Bath Road, P.O. Box 572, Roseau
Tel: 767 448 3875. Fax: 767 448 3684
Email: info@ace-engineering-ltd.com

Anthony Burnette-Biscombe
Cnr. Turkey Lane & Castle Street
P.O. Box 270, Roseau
Tel: 767 448 2896/4436
Fax: 767 448 5212
Email: larobecreole@cwdom.dm

Consulting Engineers Partnership Ltd
Jean Baptiste House, P.O. Box 117, Old
Street, Roseau
Tel: 767 448 3208/2726
Fax: 767 448 5508
Email: concept@cwdom.dm

Ocean Caraibes
P.O. Box 603, Roseau
Tel: 767 448 5962. Fax: 767 440 0464
Email: ocean@cwdom.dm

Quantity Surveying Consultants (QSC) Ltd
131 Bath Road, P.O. Box 314, Roseau
Tel: 767 448 6767. Fax: 767 448 3999
Email: qsurveying@cwdom.dm

Sorell Consulting Ltd
6 Fort Lane, P.O. Box 1232, Roseau
Tel: 767 449 9030
Fax: 767 448 1733
Email: info@sorell.dm

Surveys Unlimited
17 Church Street, P.O. Box 1915, Roseau
Tel: 767 448 1991

Transnational Engineering Consultants Inc.
Cnr Old & Church Streets, P.O. Box 2309
Roseau
Tel: 767 440 3561. Fax: 767 440 3562
Email: tec@cwdom.dm

GUESTHOUSES

Ambassador Hotel
Canefield
Tel: 449-1501. Fax: 448-5613
Email: avstoussaint@hotmail.com

Bleinheim Rainforest Island Inn
Bleinheim
Tel: 445-5588
Fax: 445-5588

Bon Marche
Roseau
Tel: 448-2083. Fax: 448-2083

Calibishie Cove
Calibishie
Tel: 265-1993
Email: covemanager@gmail.com
Email: calibishiecove@gmail.com
Website: www.calibishiecove.com

Calibishie Lodges
Calibishie
Tel: 445-8537
Email: info@calibishie-lodges.com
Website: www.calibishie-lodges.com

Carib Territory Guesthouse
Crayfish River
Tel: 445-7256
Fax: 445-7256
Email: charlohotel@yahoo.com
Website: www.avirtualdominica.com/ctgh

Chez Robar
Shawford
Tel: 449-9204. Fax: 235-5245
Email: robar@cwdom.dm
Website: www.chezrobar.com

Domcan's
Castle Bruce
Tel: 445-7794
Email: domcanrestaurant@hotmail.com
Website: www.domcansguesthouse.com

Dominica's Guesthouse
Calibishie
Tel: 445-8537
Email: info@calibishie-lodges.com
Website: www.calibishie-lodges.com

Douglas Guest House
Portsmouth
Tel: 445-5639
Email: mendoug@cwdom.dm

End of Eden
Copt Hall
Tel: 448-8272. Fax: 448-8272
Email: clemetineedwards@yahoo.com

Falls View Guesthouse
Trafalgar
Tel: 448-0064
Email: fallsview@cwdom.dm
Website: www.avirtualdominica.com/fallsv

Golden Cottage Inc
Tel: 448-3292
Email: jbe10@hotmail.com

Heaven's Best Guest House & Restaurant
Tel: 445-6677. Fax: 277-3952
Email: cleony1@hotmail.com
Website: www.heavensbestguesthouse.com

Hibiscus Valley Inn
Concord
Tel: 445-8195
Email: hibiscusvalley@hotmail.com

Home From Home
Goodwill
Tel: 449-8593
Email: lifeline@cwdom.dm
Website: www.islandguests.com

Hummingbird Inn
Canefield
Tel: 449-1042
Email: hummingbird@cwdom.dm
Email: hummingbirdinn04@yahoo.com
Website: www.thehummingbirdinn.com

Kent Antony Guesthouse
Roseau
Tel: 448-2730
Email: lovelydominica@earthlink.net

La Paz
Goodwill
Email: lapaz@cwdom.dm

Le Petit Paradis
Wotten Waven
Tel: 448-5946. Fax: 440-4352
Email: lepetitparadis200@hotmail.com

MA Bass Central Guest House
Roseau
Tel: 448-2999

Mamie's Sulphur Spring Guest House
Picard
Tel: 445-3417. Fax: 235-4476
Email: mamies@cwdom.dm

Mr Clean Bed & Breakfast
Goodwill
Tel: 440-2969
Fax: 440-2970
Email: mrcleanfed9@cwdom.dm

Narakiel's Inn
Roseau
Tel: 276-4492
Fax: 614-1328
Email: narakiels@gmail.com
Website: www.narakielsinn.com

Pepper's Cottage & Taxi Service
Mahaut/Pottersville
Tel: 245-1234
Email: peppers2day@yahoo.com
Email: askpepper@pepperscottage.com
Website: www.pepperscottage.com

Rachelles Retreat
Salisbury
Tel: 449-6262
Email: philmambo@hotmail.com

Roseau Valley
Copt Hall
Tel: 449-8176. Fax: 449-8722
Email: rosevale@cwdom.dm
Website: www.roseauvalleyhotel.com

St Aimie's Guesthouse
Elmshall
Tel: 440-4464. Fax: 448-4464
Email: sento62@hotmail.com

St James Guesthouse
Goodwill
Tel: 448-7170
Email: stjamesguesthouse@hotmail.com
Website: www.avirtualdominica.com/st-jamesguesthouse

Sea World Guesthouse
Castle Comfort
Tel: 448-5086. Fax: 448-5168
Email: seaworlddominica@yahoo.com
Website: www.avirtualdominica.com/seaworld

Sister Sea Lodges
Picard
Tel: 445-5211. Fax: 445-5211
Email: sangow@cwdom.dm
Website: www.sistersealodge.com

Springfield Guesthouse
Springfield
Tel: 449-3026
Email: nosler@clemson.edu
Website: www.springfield-dominica.org

Stonedge
Salisbury
Tel: 449-6536
Email: stonedge@free.fr

Sunrise Garden Guesthouse
Calibishie
Tel: 445-8462
Email: sargeman1@aol.com
Website: www.calibishiesunrise.com

Symes-Zee Villa
Laudat
Tel: 448-2494
Email: symes_zee@hotmail.com

Titiwi Inn
Castle Comfort
Tel: 448-0553
Email: info@titiwi.com
Website: www.titiwi.com

Wind Swept Guesthouse
Woodfordhill
Tel: 445-8982. Fax: 445-8982

Yacht Inn
Roseau
Tel: 448-3497
Email: yachtinndom@yahoo.tw

Zandoli Inn
Stowe
Tel: 446-3161. Fax: 446-3344
Email: zandoli@cwdom.dm
Website: www.zandoli.com

HOTELS

Anchorage Hotel & Dive Centre
Roseau
Tel: 448-2638. Fax: 440-2639
Email: anchorage@cwdom.dm
Website: www.anchoragehotel.dm

Beau Rive
Castle Bruce
Tel: 445-8992. Fax: 445-8992
Email: info@beaurive.com
Website: www.beaurive.com

Castle Comfort Lodge
Castle Comfort
Tel: 448-2188. Fax: 448-6088
Email: dive@cwdom.dm
Website: www.castlecomfortdivelodge.com

Comfortel De Champ
Picard
Tel: 275-3710
Email: info@godominica.com
Website: www.godominica.com

Evergreen Hotel
Castle Comfort
Tel: 448-3288
Fax: 448-6800
Email: evergreen@cwdom.dm
Website: www.avirtualdominica.com/
evergreen

Fort Young Hotel
Roseau
Tel: 448-5000
Fax: 448-5006
Email: fortyoung@cwdom.dm
Website: www.fortyounghotel.com

Garraway Hotel
Roseau
Tel: 449-8800
Fax: 449-8807
Email: garraway@cwdom.dm
Website: www.garrwayhotel.com

Jungle Bay Resort & Spa
Delices
Tel: 446-1789. Fax: 446-1090
Email: info@junglebaydominica.com
Website: www.junglebaydominica.com

Morning Bird
Mero
Tel: 449-7401
Email: morningbirdhotel@gmail.com
Website: www.morningbirdhotel.dm

Papillote Wilderness Retreat
Trafalgar
Tel: 448-2287. Fax: 448-2285
Email: papillote@cwdom.dm
Website: www.papillote.dm

Picard Beach Wellness Eco-Cottages
Picard
Tel: 445-5131. Fax: 445-5599
Email: picardbeach@cwdom.dm
Website: www.avirtualdominica.com

Pointsettia Hotel
Goodwill
Tel: 449-9428. Fax: 449-9430
Email: pointsettiahotel@cwdom.dm
Website: www.pointsettia.com

Red Rock Haven Hotel & Spa
Calibishie
Tel: 445-7997
Email: info@redrockhaven.com
Website: www.redrockhaven.com

Rosalie Bay Resorts
Rosalie
Email: gretab@rosaliebay.com
Website: www.rosaliebay.com

Roxy's Mountain Lodge
Laudat
Tel: 448-4845
Fax: 448-4845
Email: roxys@cwdom.dm
Website: www.avirtualdominica.com/
eiroxys

Silks Boutique Hotel
Hatton Garden
Tel: 445-8846
Fax: 440-4891
Email: info@silks-hotel.com
Website: www.silks-hotel.com

Sunset Bay Club & Seaside Dive Resort
Batalie
Tel: 446-6522
Fax: 446-6523
Email: sunset@cwdom.dm
Website: www.sunsetbayclub.com

Sutton Place
Roseau
Tel: 449-8700
Fax: 448-3045
Email: sutton2@cwdom.dm
Website:
www.suttonplacehoteldominica.com

Tamarind Tree Hotel
Salisbury
Tel: 449-7395
Fax: 449-7395
Email: hotel@tamarindtreedominica.com
Website: www.tamarindtreedominica.com

Vena's Paradise
Pond Casse
Tel: 449-2001
Fax: 448-0539
Email: venas@cwdom.dm
Website: www.venashotel.com

Wesleeann Suites
Canefield
Tel: 449-2473
Email: wesleeann@cwdom.dm
Email: wesleeann88@yahoo.com

LAWYERS

Anthony Astaphan
65 King George V Street, P.O. Box 75
Roseau
Tel: 767 448 3841. Fax: 767 448 0520
Email: astaphana@cwdom.dm

Mrs Singoalla Blomqvist-Williams
16 Hanover Street, P.O. Box 1671, Roseau
Tel: 767 448 0950. Fax: 767 448 0949
Email: williams@cwdom.dm

Ms Alix Boyd-Knights
14 King George V Street, Roseau
Tel: 767 448 5550. Fax: 767 448 5550
Email: kaichay@marpin.dm

Bruney's Law Offices
12 Virgin Lane, P.O. Box 2000, Roseau
Tel: 767 448 0200. Fax: 767 448 0202
Email: bruneym@cwdom.dm

Gerald D. Burton
9 Great Marlborough Street, P.O. Box 1976
Roseau
Tel: 767 449 8330. Fax: 767 449 8343
Email: burton@cwdom.dm

De Freitas & De Freitas
28 Great Marlborough Street, P.O. Box
2306, Roseau
Tel: 767 448 2530. Fax: 767 448 6760
Email: def@marpin.dm

Don Christopher & Co.
7 Cross Street, P.O. Box 210, Canefield
Tel: 767 449 0758. Fax: 767 449 0759
Email: donhimself@marpin.dm

Ms Cilma A.M. Dupigny
Van Cilclif House, 20 Hanover Street
P.O. Box 1719, Roseau
Tel: 767 448 2168. Fax: 767 448 6808
Email: dupignyc@cwdom.dm

Dyer & Dyer
19 Fields Lane, Roseau
Tel: 448 2617/449-9798. Fax: 448 7810
Email: dyer@cwdom.dm

Emanuel & Isidore
31 Great Marlborough Street, P.O. Box
2370, Roseau
Tel: 767 448 5204. Fax: 767 448 8755
Email: emanuelg@cwdom.dm
info@goneasyoffshore.com
website: www.goneasyoffshore.com

Harris & Harris
3 Hodges Lane, Roseau
Tel: 767 448 2350. Fax: 767 448 6302
Email: armhar@cwdom.dm

Alick Lawrence
Corner of Long & Hodges Lane, Roseau
Tel: 767 448 7697. Fax: 767 448 3511
Email: lawrencea@cwdom.dm

Lennox Lawrence
10 Old Street, P.O. Box 320, Roseau
Tel: 767 448 4771. Fax: 767 448 7376
Email:barrister@cwdom.dm

Gene C. Pestaina
3 Victoria Street, P.O. Box 1647, Roseau
Tel: 767 448 8687. Fax: 767 448 2978

Ashton Piper
66 Queen Mary Street, Roseau
Tel: 767 448 3149. Fax: 767 448 3149

Mrs Joan K.R. Prevost
18 Kennedy Avenue, P.O. Box 261, Roseau
Tel: 767 448 5832. Fax: 767 448 7582
Email: prevostjkr@cwdom.dm

Prevost & Williams
42 Hillsborough Street, Roseau
Tel: 767 448 2808. Fax: 767 449 8361

Serrant & Associates
33 Great George Street, 2nd Floor, P.O.
Box 658, Roseau
Tel: 767 448 6149. Fax: 767 448 0096

QUANTITY SURVEYORS

Derek Angol
P.O. Box 650, Roseau
Tel: 448 7437. Fax: 448 6002
Email: fortknox856@yahoo.com

Quantity Surveying Consultants (QSC) Ltd
131 Bath Road, P.O. Box 314, Roseau
Tel: 767 448 6767. Fax: 767 448 3999

Surveys Unlimited
2nd Floor, Woodstone Mall, Crn. Cork and
Gt. George Streets, P.O. Box 1915, Roseau
Tel: 767 448 1991. Fax: 767 448 1991

REAL ESTATE AGENTS

Casaropa Real Estate
Bay Street, Portsmouth
Tel: 767 445 5277. Fax: 767 500 4536
Email: casaropa@marpin.dm

CAS Estate Agents Ltd
131 Bath Road, P.O. Box 314, Roseau
Tel: 767 448 6767
Fax: 767 448 3999
Email: qsurveying@cwdom.dm

D.R.E.A.M.S
Calibishie, P.O. Box 2179, Roseau
Tel: 767 445 3102. Cell: 767 315 5523
Email: dominicadreams@hotmail.com
Email: uprising1@cwdom.dm

M & J Happy Home Realtors
Antrim Valley, Springfield
Tel: 767 449 2789
Email: etiennej@cwdom.dm

Riviere Real Estate International
59 King George V Street, P.O. Box 54
Roseau
Tel: 767 448 8333. Fax: 767 448 8335

Safe Haven Real Estate
P.O. Box 21, Roseau
Tel: 767 440 0878. Fax: 767 448 5338
Email: safehaven@cwdom.dm

Shillingford Estates Ltd.
Macoucherie Estate, P.O. Box 90, Roseau
Tel: 767 449 6409/6224. Fax: 767 449 6904
Email: macoucherierum@hotmail.com

SHIPPING AGENTS

Balthazar Shipping Agency
47 A Kennedy Avenue, P.O. Box 2134
Roseau
Tel: (767) 448 7523. Fax: (767) 448 7524

CIS Enterprises Ltd
54 Old Street, P.O. Box 0921, Roseau
Tel: (767) 448 0474. Fax: (767) 449 9054
Email: manager@cis.dm

CMA-CGM
Old Street, P.O. Box 771, Roseau
Tel: (767) 448 2181. Fax: (767) 448 5787

Element Agencies
Woodbridge Bay, P.O. Box 2266, Roseau
Tel: (767) 448 6666
Fax: (767) 440 3459

H D L Services
75 Hillsborough Street
Roseau
Tel: (767) 440 0312
Fax: (767) 500 0312
Website: www.hdlservices.com

Jno Baptiste A D Shipping & Customs
Brokers
Ground Floor Prevost Cinemall
Kennedy Avenue
P.O. Box 1926
Roseau
Tel: (767) 440 3930
Fax: (767) 440 3930

Network Trading Inc.
35 Goodwill Road, Pottersville, P.O. Box
1727, Roseau
Tel: (767) 440 4073. Fax: (767) 440 4679
Email: manager@ntidominica.com

O.D. Brisbane & Sons
Canefield, P.O. Box 145, Roseau
Tel: (767) 448 2087. Fax: (767) 448 5609
Email: odbrisbane@cwdom.dm

Shillingford A.C & Co. Ltd
King George V Street, P.O. Box 123
Roseau
Tel: (767) 448 2481. Fax: (767) 448 6681
Email: acs@cwdom.dm

SHIPPING COMPANIES

B & J Shipping
47-B Kennedy Avenue, Roseau
Tel: (767) 449 8724. Fax: (767) 449 8724

Econocaraibe Consolidators Inc.
H.H.V Whitchurch & Co. Ltd.
Old Street
P.O. Box 771
Roseau
Tel: (767) 448 2181
Fax: (767) 448 5787

Geest Line Ltd.
Old Street
P.O. Box 771
Roseau
Tel: (767) 448 2181
Fax: (767) 448 5787

Grace Hill Shipping
Grandby Street
Portsmouth
Tel: (767) 445 4391
Fax: (767) 445 6423

Grace Hill Shipping & Marketing Services
56 Potters Street
Pottersville
Roseau
Tel: (767) 448 6166

Tropical Shipping
Goodwill Road, P.O. Box 21
Roseau
Tel: (767) 448 1744z
Fax: (767) 448 7877
Website: www.tropical.com

Wyllis Services
20 Bath Road & Deep Water Harbour
P.O. Box 443, Roseau
Tel: (767) 448 3911/ 448 4384
Fax: (767) 448 4528